Storyteller Media and its logo are trademarks of Storyteller Media LLC, a joint venture with Gungnir Entertainment LLC, and the literary company of Curiosity Entertainment LLC

Publisher and wholesale inquiries: Storyteller Media, www.storyteller.media

Cover design by Ben Ceccarelli
Book layout design by Mohamed Samah

ISBN 9798999529978

Edited by Charles Allen

Publisher and wholesale enquiries:
www.storyteller.media

Distributed by macmillan

Printed in China

First Edition: 2026

YOU DON'T KNOW DICK

HOW I HEALED MY DADDY ISSUES FIXING BROKEN DICKS

BY

KIRSTINA DENTON

STORYTELLER MEDIA

For Dad.
Thank you. I love you. I miss you.

PROLOGUE
I DIDN'T KNOW DICK

"Almost every hand you have ever shaken has had a dick in it."

—Rusafu

Small dicks. Big dicks. Scared dicks. Scarred dicks. Crooked dicks. Confused dicks. Colorful dicks. Is that a dick? Long dicks. Short dicks. That-looks-like-fun dicks. Poor dicks. Rich dicks. That-is-just-art dicks. Famous dicks. Lonely dicks. Smelly dicks. Friendly dicks. Do you even have a dick because I can't find it? Dicks. Hundreds of dicks and all with one thing in common… they were broken. And it was my job to fix them.

The "fixing" I'm talking about was purely clinical. No, I wasn't a sex worker or a porn star or even the high-end escort my mom thought I should've been typecast as, even if I almost accidentally became one of those, too. Yes, I spent an entire year of my life legally fixing hundreds of broken dicks. While this unique day job instantly made me the most interesting person at any dinner table, the job eventually blew up my life—forever changing the way I see men, and naturally, their dicks.

I didn't plan on becoming a dick fixer. I started as an office manager, helping a small wellness clinic get off the ground in Los Angeles, which, for anonymity and just a dash of mystery, I'll simply call The Clinic. The city was already bursting with wellness centers, day spas, and anti-aging clinics in every strip mall, all claiming to be the answer to people's existential dread. Our budding clinic needed an edge, something to set us apart.

One Joe Rogan podcast later, The Clinic's owner had a grand idea: save the dicks, save The Clinic. He was practically bouncing with excitement when he pitched it to me.

"Dude, there's this machine you put on your dick," he said, eyes shining. "And it shocks it back to life."

I smirked, wondering if he was serious. "Does it work?" I asked, humoring him. He shrugged. "Guys care about two things: their hair and their dicks. They'll spend a fortune to keep both thick, full and shining."

I didn't share his excitement, but fascination pulled me in. Curiosity followed. And more than anything, I hoped this would bankroll my real dream of becoming a working actor/writer in Hollywood.

The next thing I knew, I was on a plane to Tucson, Arizona, headed for a seminar that would certify me in Extracorporeal Shockwave Therapy for Erectile Dysfunction. Fancy name, right? The machine once pulverized kidney stones but now promised to spark blood flow and repair tissue when applied to the right spot. I still thought the whole thing was ridiculous, but in my head, I was already rehearsing the "you'll never believe this" story. "How was your weekend, Kristina?" "Oh, I just attended a dick-fixing certification workshop. Yours?"

So there I sat in the desert, in a dimly lit resort ballroom, surrounded by urologists and doctors from across the country. A projector blasted a massive cross-section of male anatomy on the wall for our reference. Imagine a dick and balls blown up to the size of a small, but aggressive SUV. I flashed back to high school freshman human biology class where my teacher screamed "PENIS!" at the top of her lungs on day one. I assume it was to desensitize us to the technically accurate, yet appropriately comical language we would be hearing from her for the next year. Or, maybe, she was testing our maturity level. We failed, hard.

Clinical dick words now poured from the shockwave instructor like a symphony, washing over a room full of urologists who paid their mortgages with penises and the diseases that wrecked them. By "what the fuck am I doing here?" moment number four, I realized I might be the only one internally giggling. We were literally being trained to point a gun-like machine at a broken dick and charging for it. Absurd. But these doctors nodded along as if it were gospel. There was a culture, a community, a whole industry of professional dick saviors. Who knew? Not me.

After hours of lectures, it was time for the "hands-on" portion. Oh God, really? Right in the center of the room lay a volunteer; a doctor in his sixties who looked just like the Santa from the mall in my childhood Christmas pictures. His poor pensive Santa shlong covered by a mere thin white medical drape, anxiously waited for us trainees to get in there and practice on him. I watched as the other attendees approached, impersonal and detached, handling his dick like there wasn't a human on the other side of it.

Finally, my turn. Terrified, I took a breath, leaned over, and surprised both of us as I blurted out, "Hi, how are you?"

Santa blinked, caught off guard, clearly not expecting the pleasantries. "Oh, uh…fine, thanks."

We shared an awkward laugh, and then I reached for his… well, you know… worried little wiener.

His cold, lubed-up piece of flesh slid into my palm, limp as the world's saddest hot dog. I fired up the shockwave machine, and the jackhammering whir rattled my bones. Oh, the things I do for rent money. Even more scared, I pressed the futuristic, gun shaped wand onto his lifeless Christmas stocking dick and braced for the scream. Nothing. Instead, he laid motionless and unbothered by me zapping the most sensitive real estate on his body.

My wrist trembled. Was it the machine vibrating or my nerves? The instructor jolted me out of my trance. "Move the wand. There's a lot to cover."

Right. I had to accomplish something, even if this felt like a prank on a twisted game show. I was there to shock this man's dick back to life.

Thanks to the relentless work ethic I inherited from my parents, equal parts grit and stubbornness disguised as ambition, I refused to fail. At the time, I had no clue just how successful I'd one day become in this new, weird world of fixing dicks I'd discovered. But I knew I'd make my mama proud, one perked up pickle at a time.

The conference delivered all sorts of not-so-useful, but fascinating tidbits, like the medical reasons why dicks age, suffer, and die. Or why pills and injections were not enough to resolve the male erectile dysfunction epidemic. Or even the idea that men might go to more extreme lengths to save their dicks than women do to save their faces. Well, that might be a stretch, but you get the idea.

I thought I knew what I was getting myself into. I thought this quirky job would provide me with a lifetime of wild stories to shock my friends with at brunch or just be an odd way to pay the bills while I pursued my real dreams. But the truth? I didn't know dick. Not only did this job make me more money than any job I'd ever had and expose me to more dicks than I'd ever thought I'd see, but it came at a time in my life when I needed it most. That year I didn't just refurbish dicks; I deconstructed the male ego. The Clinic became my spiritual classroom where I began to untangle the most complicated relationship I'd ever had with any dick—the one with my father.

This story is how I healed my daddy issues: by fixing broken dicks.

CHAPTER 1
DICK FIXER

"Even the world's greatest actor cannot fake an erection."
—Mokokoma Mokhonoana

When I got certified in Extracorporeal Shockwave Therapy for Erectile Dysfunction, I still had no idea what this job actually looked like in practice. *Okay, so random strangers were gonna come into The Clinic, lie down, and pay me to fix their dicks?* Cool. So what did that make me? A dick fixer? Hilarious.

I remember coining that title for myself. "Dick Fixer" felt bold, catchy, and weirdly... empowering? When I mentioned it to friends, each one replied with some variation of, "Ohh, that makes so much sense." Their responses were code for: You've always been a little sleaze-adjacent, Kristina. We've been waiting for this moment your whole life.

I have to admit, my friends had me pegged, like fortune-tellers who didn't need crystal balls to predict I'd end up surrounded by dicks. I've always been comfortable talking about sex, maybe a little too comfortable. Cracking open taboo topics, playing with the edges of discomfort, and turning shame into a punchline... that's my shit. I flirt with life for sport. According to all the birth charts that my mathematician-turned-astrologer step-grandfather interpreted for me, stirring the pot is in my cosmic DNA. So yeah, locking me in a room with broken penises and fragile male egos felt like a natural career move, or at least, it'd be a hell of a story to tell my grandkids one day.

But before we go, ahem, balls deep into this story, let me back up to the month leading up to this job: It was an absolute shitshow. I was five years into a long-term relationship with a guy we'll call Z. His real name was long and tough to say, so he preferred his nickname. We lived together, shared bank accounts, and rescued two dogs, Sam and Gus, who were basically our children. Gus just started having seizures which turned out to be epilepsy. On top of that, Z's mom was diagnosed with breast cancer. Then Z got hit by a car, right after being fired from his six-figure job that paid most of our bills.

So yeah. Things were going great.

Then as if the universe needed any more fuel for the dumpster fire that was my life, I was also waiting for a particularly devastating phone call. The kind of call you know is coming but still lands like a punch to the gut. My dad was fifty-nine years old and dying of terminal prostate cancer. His cancer had slowly been destroying him for the last three and a half years.

Less than a week after I returned to L.A., freshly certified in Extracorporeal Shockwave Therapy for Erectile Dysfunction, my sister, Lucy, called me at work on a Monday evening. I think I was mid-dick joke when I picked up the phone.

Her voice was tight, calm and pointed, but she held it together enough to say, "It's time, Kris."

She didn't need to say more. I knew.

I sucked in a sharp breath. "Okay."

"He's in the hospital. It's not good. Just... It's time. They think only a couple days now."

Oh, shit. Not a countdown. That's um... I wasn't ready for that. It felt like whiplash going from dick doctoring to my dad dying in a few days. My nervous system had no clue how to process those back-to-back realities. The walls of The Clinic collapsed toward me.

But I did what I always did as the oldest daughter of four girls: I comforted Lucy, steadied my voice, made sure I sounded reliable to show up. My feelings could wait, per usual.

"Okay. I'll be there as soon as I can."

"I think you should leave now. Like tonight."

I reminded Lucy that I had to pick up Grandma, my father's mother. She wouldn't be able to make it into L.A. on the train from San Diego until tomorrow afternoon, so I would have to wait. Lucy didn't like the sound of that, but she understood.

I hung up and locked into the protocol I knew too well: just keep moving. Turn off the difficult feelings. Execute the mission instead: our family motto.

Telling my bosses the situation was peak surrealism. "Hey, I can't fix dicks just yet. I gotta go bury my dad. Well, he's not dead yet, but... he's close and I should probably say goodbye first. So, can I get a few days off to deal with that?"

They looked at me with faces full of sympathy that I didn't want. They didn't know my dad. They didn't know how complicated his death was. It wasn't a Hallmark moment; this was the man I'd spent most of my life resenting. The man who scared me, disappointed me, and somehow still managed to make me feel worthless in his eyes.

So instead of bringing dicks back to life, I had to go help put one down.

I told my bosses I wouldn't be gone long because God forbid if they thought I wasn't committed. I needed this job. I needed the money, and I needed something solid on the other side of the worst moment of my life. Even if that something was a room full of sad dicks and medical-grade lube.

I don't even remember how I got home that night. I was already in such a daze. I stared at my closet like it was written in another language. How do you choose an outfit for your father's funeral when he's still breathing? I just kept thinking: this is so fucked.

The phone rang all night; the shrill tone sliced through every attempt at silence. My family, mostly women, spun around in an anxiety cyclone of updates, coordination, and emotional ping-pong. We're not good with quiet. We fill every pause with noise, finding comfort in knowing we're on the same page.

My mom called me from the hospital. "I'm here with your dad. I'm going to put him on the phone now."

My gut reaction, "No, Mom. I don't want to talk to him."

And I didn't. I never did. I'd spent decades dodging conversations with this man, on the phone and in person, and now I was supposed to perform closure. Fuck off.

But she handed my dad the phone anyway.

"Hey, big girl," he said, voice thin and trembling.

Fuck. He sounds small. Not scary. Not angry. Just... dying.

My whole body locked up, bracing for impact. But instead of telling him all the things I'd rehearsed for years, I defaulted to comfort.

"I'm coming tomorrow, okay? Around 6:30. I'm bringing Grandma. Just... don't forget. 6:30. Okay, Dad? I need you to know the time. Okay?"

I don't know why I said that. Maybe part of me thought if I told him exactly when I'd be there, he'd hold on long enough for us to make it.

By then, he couldn't walk or bathe himself. My other sister, Lily, God bless her, had been taking care of him and told me he'd made her re-wash his dick, balls, butthole, and taint if she didn't do it to his standards. We laughed about it. Of course he did. The man was meticulous until the end.

"I don't know how else to say this to you, babe, but I'm gonna need you to wash my taint. You gotta do it." He'd scoff at Lily from his shower chair.

That night, the updates kept coming. His breathing worsened. An ambulance rushed him to the hospital because his lungs had filled with fluid. The Emergency Room doctors wanted to drain his lungs, but his platelet count had crashed and was too low to successfully complete the procedure. Platelets are tiny blood cells that help your body form clots. Without enough of them, even the tiniest pinprick could cause dangerous bleeding.

"So he's just going to drown?" My lips quivered with rage. No one had an answer.

I sat there, numb, furious, devastated and haunted by the thought of my dad's body betraying him in slow motion. So cruel.

This ending wasn't how I'd imagined it. Not that I ever pictured the way my dad would die or that he would die at all, but so painfully? He was too young to die. I was too young for a dead dad. Plus, I was too consumed by surviving my own life to imagine his ending.

That also wasn't how I envisioned the start of my dick-fixing career. The funny job that promised to save The Clinic had to be put on hold for my dad before it even began. The man who had consumed so much of my life with fear, resentment, and longing took center stage once again. My dad always managed to suck the air out every room, even if his lungs were failing. And if he hadn't been my dad, and my mom didn't guilt me into tolerating him, I would have said goodbye after high school and never looked back.

CHAPTER 2
MY FIRST DICK

"The best way to avoid dicks: Don't be one."

—Mark B. Borg Jr., Don't Be a Dick: Change Yourself, Change Your World

I'll get back to dicks shortly, but first, some context on the original one.

The first dick in my life was, naturally, my dad. And yes, you can read that literally or metaphorically, but it's mostly the latter. Like most fathers, he was my first blueprint for men. Without ever meaning to, or making an effort, he taught me everything I would come to believe about them; whether they were safe, whether they could be trusted, whether they'd be allies or adversaries. Spoiler: the blueprint was more of a demolition plan than an architectural sketch.

So, you can imagine the manual on men I had walking into The Clinic. Not great.

My parents met when my dad was twenty-two and my mom was thirty-one. That's right, mama snagged herself a hot, younger man. She was a babe. He was a stud and probably just horny. Six months later, they were pregnant with me. Three years and four daughters later, they didn't stand a chance.

My dad was twenty-six, with four girls under the age of four. A literal man-child trying to raise children, while still being a kid himself. That's the kind version of the story. The more accurate version?

My father was an angry, unpredictable, alcoholic narcissist who verbally, and sometimes physically, abused us. Or at least that one time when I was nine and he threw me down the hallway. Hard to forget that moment in my formative years. My dad was mostly absent, and when he wasn't, we never knew which version of him would show up, fun dad or raging asshole.

The inconsistency made for an unstable house built on fear, yelling, and resentment with a few well-timed jokes to survive the chaos.

Naturally, this set me up for a glowing track record in adult relationships.

There were years of seeking validation. Wild codependency. A deep, haunting belief that I had no inherent worth unless someone else, usually a man, reflected it back to me. I dated addicts, liars, violent narcissists, emotionally unavailable boyfriends I thought I could rescue. It was like auditioning new versions of my dad on a loop, hoping one of them would stick the landing, and finally choose me.

And through it all, I heard his voice, always slurred at the edges, "Who the fuck do you think you are?"

No one, Dad. I'm no one.

So when he died, you'd think I'd feel peace. Or rage. But what I actually felt... was confusion.

I remember the flight back to L.A. I'd stayed an extra week to help my mom with logistics. She was grieving hard, even though their marriage had long since turned into a contempt-filled business partnership. She had lost her partner, the father of her kids, and the ghost who'd haunted her bedroom and wellbeing for 35 years.

And on that flight home, it hit me: the monster of my life was gone. Gone, gone. Never again, gone. And I didn't know how to feel. There was grief, sure. But there was also something else. Something harder to name... relief.

My dad couldn't hurt me anymore. No more surprise verbal assaults on me or my mom that I'd have to defend. No more insults dressed as jokes. No more walking on eggshells, praying I wouldn't be the target that day. His voice might still live in my head, but he was done adding to the script.

I was free. And then... the gut punch. Now our relationship would never get better.

There would never be a redemption arc. No final monologue where my dad took accountability, said he was sorry, told me I was worthy and lovable and swore he'd always protect me. The hope I had clung to for decades, that one day he'd look at me and say, "I'm proud of you" and mean it, was gone. No. That hope died with him.

I hadn't realized how much of my identity was tied up in that inner tug-of-war; my fear of my dad and the hope he might change. I had lived inside that tension so long, I didn't know who I was without it.

Who was I if I wasn't proving him wrong? If I wasn't fighting to be seen, to be better than he believed I was? Without that resistance, I felt... empty. No purpose. No villain. No shadow to escape from.

And then the most twisted thing of all happened. I realized right there, sitting crammed in that crusty coach window seat on the cheapest flight I could find, that I missed the monster.

CHAPTER 3
TO DICK OR NOT TO DICK

"Just at the age when you finally learn to trust yourself, you stop trusting your dick."

—Me, based on research

After my dad's funeral, I came back to The Clinic dead inside. Grief came at me like a rabid animal trapped in a cage within my soul, ripping and gnawing until there was nothing left but bone. My dad had just died, but I hadn't processed it. I hadn't cried. I wasn't numb, exactly, I was cracked open. My vulnerability was exposed, impossible to hide. My raw emotions boiling beneath the surface, desperate for an escape hatch. But now it was time for dick fixing.

I wasn't sure if the novelty had worn off or if I was just spiraling into a void of existential dread, but nothing felt funny anymore—not even penises. And that's saying something, because penises are always funny. Like have you seen them? Penises, no matter the size or shape, are these accidental protrusions off a perfectly sculpted specimen. The anxiety men must feel always guarding their penis. Poor Michaelangelo was forced to include David's penis on that incredible work of art. It wasn't his choice. It is like the OG penis designer just landed on a prototype of man that nobody improved and released it into the world to flop around, hoping no one would notice. I noticed. I always noticed.

Despite my feelings on the penis design flaw, my first client was already booked.

While I was gone saying goodbye to my father, The Clinic owners had prepped the space, purchased the dick-fixing machine, and started marketing the new service. Appointments were lined up. All I had to do was show up and pretend I knew what I was doing. Step in the room and be the confident, clinical dick whisperer they'd hired me to be. But how?

Z, my boyfriend, was being great, actually. However, he was much more emotional than me in the aftermath, which I hated. He wasn't even close to my dad. I mean, I wasn't either in my adulthood. But watching him cry over a man I'd spent a lifetime afraid of made me want to crawl out of my skin.

I didn't know how to process male vulnerability, especially when it wasn't about me. Especially when it wasn't sexy. Watching Z mourn my father felt like watching someone grieve a childhood hero who'd never knew their name. I wanted to respect it. I just didn't. In fact, I despised him for it.

"Why are you crying? Stop making this about you. He was my dad."

I was awful to Z in my grief. Then came the kicker.

A week after the funeral home turned my dad to ash, I found myself half-naked in a paper gown at a low budget imaging clinic, waiting for a mammogram. A friend had warned me that several women we knew from our old workplace were getting diagnosed with breast cancer in their 30s, so she told me to get screened. I'd set the appointment before my dad died and had entirely forgotten about it until I received the reminder text. Fuck.

I didn't have health insurance. My employer didn't offer benefits and Z was still unemployed. So I found a low-cost clinic, walked in, and sat in a cold waiting room next to three other women in hospital gowns. I felt like we were lining up for a game show, except the prize was getting your tits squished. Then I remembered that stat, one in four women will get breast cancer in their lifetime. There were four of us. I loved this moment for us.

As I waited, I thought about my dad, how many times he'd sat in waiting rooms, knowing he was dying. The rooms were stark and depressing with their shitty fluorescent overhead lighting. Dress them up however you want, they still sucked.

A tech swept in and ushered me to the exam room. Before so much as a hello, she grabbed my boobs like stress balls on sale and started pushing and prodding my breast tissue with her cold ass hands. *Did this woman get her gloves from the damn freezer?* My nipples snapped to attention like they were showing up for their first day of boot camp. Iced latex gloves plus the desert-dry AC blasting the table will do that. Then the Ice Queen slapped a small sticker on my left breast and said, "Okay, you're all set."

I didn't know the protocol, but I gave this tech zero stars for bedside manner.

"Great. Thanks."

The next tech took me into the room with the booby scanner. She wrestled my itty-bitty titty committee boobs into the high tech, yet still medieval looking torture device. The plates clamped down, flattening me like a waffle press. It hurt like a bitch. There's got to be a better way. This felt straight-up antiquated. One hard smash per boob and the mammogram was over?

I'd never had a mammogram before. I was too young. Breast cancer screenings were an old lady thing for like when people are over 40. I was in complete denial that the number was only five years away for me. I had too many things left to accomplish to admit that I was almost middle-aged. I hadn't been married, hadn't had kids, hadn't been able to sustain my life financially as a working artist. I didn't have time for this shit.

I changed back into my clothes and went to the front desk to check out. "We'll need you to come back," the receptionist said without looking up from her computer screen.

"I'm sorry, what?" My eyes widened.

"We need a closer look. Can you come in on Wednesday?"

It was Saturday. "Wait. Did they find something?"

"We don't know. It's just what the notes say."

"Is that routine?"

"Only when they see something they don't like."

The receptionist shrugged many times. Cool. I pretended to be fine with this vague, casually delivered medical cliffhanger.

Is that what the sticker on my left boob was for? It wasn't the scratch and sniff sticker I was used to getting from a doctor as a kid. I can still smell that fake-ass strawberry scent. You Were Berry Good. This was berry bad.

I walked to my car in a daze. My stomach dropped. Was I going to vomit? I drove home with a pit in my chest, a rock in my throat and a potential lump in my boob. I didn't want to tell anyone that I could possibly have breast cancer. My mom had just buried her husband. My sisters were barely hanging on. There was no room for another crisis in my family. Plus, I was the rock of our family: the one who stayed grounded in crisis, holding it together for everyone else. What the hell is the family supposed to do if the rock crumbles? Again, I had no time for my own health disaster.

I went to pick up Z from the gym and knew I had to tell him. I had to tell someone. The 30-minute drive to the gym gave me enough time to freak out and run forty-five different scenarios of how I would relay the information and how Z would respond.

I'll never forget the look on Z's face—frozen. Like he couldn't even process the words. His mom was battling breast cancer. My dad had just died. Our dog Gus's seizures were getting worse. We were maxed out. He couldn't take on one more thing. So he didn't.

"I can't hear that right now. I'm sorry. I just can't."

I couldn't blame him.

At home, I stared at myself in the mirror and saw hives all over my left breast. Anticipatory anxiety is a bitch. Residue from the sticker clung to my skin. Stress hives and gross medical adhesive that I couldn't get off. Cool. All I could think about was my left breast. Why would cancer want my boobs? They're barely there. I forced myself in the shower and silently cried, imagining myself bald. My God, I would look terrible, not hot like some women who elected to shave their heads. I was not Demi Moore in GI Jane. I couldn't pull that look off.

And fun fact: I was born with a fractured skull. The new-to-delivering-babies-doctor tried to turn me over in the birth canal with those damn antiquated forceps and BAM, the whole left side of my tiny head was crushed. I barely survived that nearly fatal mistake at one day old. Now, the left side of my head still looks like the Rocky Mountains after the apocalypse. There is no pulling off sexy baldness for this head. Not a chance.

I remembered the way my dad never lost his hair through chemo. How proud he was of that. I'd even asked the hospice nurse to cut a lock of it for my mom moments after he'd died. Everyone thought I was crazy, but she still has it. It made sense to me to preserve something he was so proud of at that moment.

That night, I couldn't sleep. I couldn't eat. My whole chest itched with anxiety. I kept thinking, "I can't be a pink-ribbon person. I hate running. I only run in emergencies now, like trying to save a dog from getting hit by a car type shit. Not for fun, not even for a good cause. I can't do a fucking 5K for my tits. I'll never make it."

A few days later, the call came. I was at The Clinic, trying to distract myself with paperwork, when the imaging center left me a voicemail.

"We found a mass. It appears to be metastasized. We need you to get an ultrasound immediately."

Excuse me? You leave that kind of message on a fucking voicemail?

I called back. They were closed. What kind of emotional drive-by bull-shit was that?

That night, I was furious. At the breast clinic. At my dad. At cancer. At everything.

I think I spent all night researching. I pulled out everything I remembered from college about finding reliable sources online. I wanted double-blind peer-reviewed studies that confirmed or denied what I was going through. None of that online WebMD bullshit. I was smarter than that. Better than that. I'd gone to college for nearly seven years, studying Exercise Science and Nutrition and had a two-year degree in Acting. I was well-educated, highly resourced and basically a non-professional investigator. If there was any explanation for a growing lump in my breast that didn't involve the "C" word, I was going to find it. I was determined to beat uncertainty.

Two days later, I was back in the doctor's office. Same paper gown. Same stupid "Hang in there!" motivational posters with cartoon ducks wearing headscarves. I wanted to punch every single one and I'm vegan. But fuck those ducks.

I waited so long to be seen, I started doodling in the little journal I always kept in my purse for stress relief. For some reason, I drew my dad. Even in the midst of awaiting my own pending doom, I thought of him first. I drew him as I remembered him most: on the golf course, a lit cigarette in one hand, the other hand raised in an "I love you" in sign language.

That was the last image I had of my dad the summer before he died. I was home for the Fourth of July, and he limped his way out to the driveway to send me off. I looked back and saw him waving goodbye with that same "I love you" sign language sendoff wave he always did. That's the last time I saw him standing.

I finished the drawing just before the tech came in and started yet another scan. After 72 hours of Googling breast-cancer ultrasounds, I was convinced I could detect it myself. I knew what I was looking for on the screen. I was practically an honorary radiologist.

As I cranked my head to see the screen, the tech squinted, "Huh. That's strange."

Pro Tip: Do not say "that's strange" unless you're a magician or an alien. And not during a breast scan where you're checking for fucking cancer.

Without a word, the tech left the room.

This place was definitely getting zero stars from me. Maybe half a star for decor. I'm sure somebody liked those ducks.

Again, I thought of my dad. And then suddenly, he appeared to me, like some weird LSD visual gone wrong. Right there in that fucking duck room, my dead dad was there. The fuck? He sucked on a cig and blew the smoke away, all cool and confident like he always did. If you asked GenAI to generate a middle-aged white dude who looked cool while smoking... Robert Denton, ladies and gentlemen.

Through the smoke he shrugged, "Babe, you're gonna be fine. Come on. You're a Denton. We're always fine."

Umm okay, Dad. How'd that work out for you?

I was arguing with my imagination, but still it felt comforting that he was there, even if I really hated the ducks now.

The tech reentered the room. "Yeah. So... it looks like the radiologist read your image wrong. He mistook your nipple for a mass. You're fine."

I stared at her. Processing. "My... nipple?"

"Yep. You're good to go."

I wanted that radiologist's name, address, children's school, and list of household pets so I could personally introduce him to his own terror spiral. But instead, I just nodded, trying to hold back my rage. "Well, that sucks. I just spent nearly a week thinking I had breast cancer and my dad just died of cancer."

"Oh, yeah. It happens."

Does it, Gina? Does it just happen? You regularly put people through hell and back by mistake? Maybe be better at your job. Just because you're immune to giving people bad news, doesn't mean I should be able to tolerate your shitty behavior or your shitty ducks!

I walked out of the doctor's office half-relieved and half-shattered.

My dad had just died of cancer. And for five days, I'd thought I'd had it too. And now? Now I had to go fix someone's dick like none of it had happened. *Wait, how big are my nipples? Are they too big? No, not now.* I would solve the nipple crisis later, probably with my expert Google research skills.

The morning of my first appointment, I showed up late. Typical. My daily Uber took forever to arrive. I'd sold my car to fund a short film, so rideshare drivers were now my unofficial coworkers. I used to joke that I had a chauffeur, which made the seven-minute ride to work feel a little more glamorous than it was. Every ride was a micro-adventure with a new stranger, and honestly, I needed the distraction from my grief. The passivity of riding in a car, maybe the quiet or a song that would play, always stirred feelings. I'd rather talk to randos then process my emotions.

So, I arrived late: flustered, apologetic and full of shame. The Clinic owner looked up from the desk as I entered and said, "He's already in the room. And... you might know him." Apparently, he was semi-famous. They said the patient's name, and I immediately recognized it.

Perfect. Let's add pressure to the pile, shall we?

Heart pounding, I tossed my purse behind the front desk and headed toward the treatment room. I walked down the hallway that separated the entrance to the room from the actual treatment area. From there, I saw two large feet dangling off the edge of the table, and patterned dress socks stretched over long, hairy legs.

Socks say a lot about a man. He either picked them with intention or threw on the first clean pair he found. My clients all had sock stories. Weirdly, they became my first impression. My personal intake form for the kind of man I would spend six sessions with.

My eyes followed the socks up to the legs and the paper drape barely covered the man's crotch. Tom, let's call him that, lay flat on his back, scrolling through his phone like this appointment was a routine dental cleaning. And there it was: my first paying penis.

Sorry, I had to break from "dick" because I liked the alliteration. It won't happen again.

I swallowed hard. "Hi, I'm Kristina. I'll be working with you today." I flashed a polite smile; the kind I used to serve tables and fake orgasms. The kind of smile you give when your father's body has just been turned to ash and you're still not sure if this job is a nervous breakdown or divine intervention.

Tom barely glanced up. I could feel his nerves vibrating off him. Mine were worse, trapped in a satin blouse already damp with sweat. Satin. For my first day of dick duty. What the fuck had I been thinking?

I snapped on a pair of latex gloves with all the elegance of someone trying to open a pickle jar with wet hands. Tom asked something, but my brain, mid-panic, missed it.

Oh fuck. Oh fuck. What the fuck am I doing here?

I stared at the paper drape. *Don't stare at his dick. Don't be a creep. He's just a man. A sad man. With a sad dick. Who probably already hates you. It's just skin, Kristina. Grow the fuck up.*

Tom kept his eyes glued to his phone like this wasn't the strangest thing that had ever happened to either of us.

"How are you today, Tim?" I chirped in my most cheerful customer service voice.

"It's Tom."

Shit. "Tom, sorry!" *Nailed it.*

I wheeled the shockwave machine closer to Tom's body and flipped it on. It whirred like it was warming up for battle, absolutely no help to either of us.

"How long will this take?" he asked.

"About 45 minutes," I answered, wondering if that was correct.

Tom let out a long, annoyed sigh. "And it works, right?"

"There are a lot of studies..."

"I mean in your experience. With your clients."

Oh God. How the fuck should I know, Tom? You're my first dick, man. No one told you this. You're my first. Fuck, that doesn't sound promising. No one wants to be the first.

I smiled. "No complaints so far."

He scoffed. I tried not to take it personally.

Then with all the grace of a baby deer on roller skates, I peeled back the paper drape.

There it was. A stranger's dick. Flaccid. Lifeless. And looking for answers.

I tried to look away but couldn't. It looked... normal. I mean, older. But still.

Was this the oldest dick I'd ever seen? Should I be keeping track of these dicks like a weird reverse sex list? Shut up, Kristina.

"It's cold in here," Tom muttered. Cue the male-ego defense.

"Sorry about that." Cue me taking responsibility for The Clinic's thermostat.

I grabbed the ultrasound gel and squeezed. The bottle farted, loud. Of course it did.

I swallowed the giggle and kept my face clinical. *Normalize the fart. Be the professional.* I worked the gel between my gloved palms like I was plotting a murder. I'd never touched a penis clinically before. Not like this. Not under fluorescent lighting.

This gel was basically lube, right? How do you put lube on a stranger's dick and make it not sexual? Thanks for nothing, Dave-from-training.

Oh my God. I'm drooling. Why am I drooling? Is this like some Pavlovian response?! If a penis gets this close to my mouth, does my brain think I need to put it in there? This is NOT your penis to please, Kristina! Why don't we have face masks? God, I'm the worst. What am I doing here?!

I made a crab claw with my hand and picked up the shaft like it was a rare museum artifact. Gentle. No, aggressive. Aggressive is medical. Right?

Just don't stroke it. And don't curl your fingers. Gripping is for handjobs. Not for this.

Suddenly, and thankfully, I remembered when you feed a horse you flatten your palm against its mouth, so it won't bite you. Somehow, the connection made absolute sense to me at this moment. For the first time in my life, I felt grateful for growing up in the country with horse friends. So, I flattened both my palms and slapped the gel on like I was making a mayonnaise sandwich. Gross, yes. But sexual? No. I stayed in the non-sexual, clinical safe zone where there would be no chance or thought of happy endings.

Tom flinched. I froze. He could feel that.

Oh God. He can feel me touching him. Is he turned on? I don't know. His dick's broken. Oh look, pubic hair goes gray. Fuck.

I wiped my gloves with a Kleenex. It disintegrated. Now my hands were covered in sticky gel and tissue lint. *Awesome.*

I peeled off the gloves, gel smeared all over my forearms. Ew. I tossed that pair and grabbed another set. I was basically an amateur magician at this point, pulling anxiety out of thin air.

"Okay," I said. "This might hurt a bit."

I picked up the gun shaped wand, pressed it right into Tom's fretful shaft and pulled the trigger. The machine jackhammered to life, sending forceful sound waves into Tom's dick.

"Wait!"

I jumped and killed the machine's switch. Tom wasn't in pain. He was crying. My hand froze mid-air.

"Did I hurt you?"

"No... no." He looked away, ashamed. "Can you just... give me a minute?"

I nodded, set the wand down, and turned to leave.

"Don't go," he said quickly. "Please."

I paused.

"I forgot how to do this," he whispered.

"Do what?"

He swallowed. "I haven't had another woman see me like this in forty years. Just her. Diane. And now she's gone. Don't ever get cancer, okay? It's fucking brutal."

His words sliced through me.

"Everyone says I should start dating again. That I'm not dead yet. But I don't want time. I want her. I should be dead. Not her."

I didn't speak. I let him talk.

"I feel selfish for wanting to move on. But Diane? She'd want me flirting with every woman I could find. She was like that. She had a big spirit." He chuckled, despite himself. "Like I'm a catch at my age. Look at me. Jesus. Don't get old either, alright? It's awful."

I smiled, charmed. Handed him a tissue. Not the dirty one. A clean one. I'm not an animal.

"I tried," he continued. "I joined that ridiculous dating site for people my age. Met some nice women. Even liked one of them. But every time I get close to someone, I think of Diane. And this guy..." He pointed to his penis, continuing, "Acts like I forgot him at home. Like he's still hibernating. Useless."

He exhaled hard. "I just need some reassurance. That maybe there's a chance. That if I'm going to stick around, maybe I can feel alive again. I've got kids. Grandkids. I don't want to miss that. But it's hard. Or not hard, in my case."

He pointed again. "I'm sorry," he blubbered. "I don't mean to overshare."

"Don't worry," I said.

"I just... I need this to work. You're the expert. Tell me it will. Tell me it's going to be okay. I need a win here, Kristina."

He looked at me like I was holding a miracle in my latex-covered hands. And as my heart pounded in my chest, I realized something: This job was never just going to be about dicks.

Grief is weird like that. One minute you're staring out an airplane window, wondering who you are without your lifelong antagonist, and the next, you're back in L.A., slipping on latex gloves, and holding a stranger's dick like it's a sacred relic. There's no gentle re-entry. No soft landing. Just a paper gown, a bottle of farting gel, and a man named Tom with a limp dick and a broken heart, looking to me for answers I didn't even have for myself.

CHAPTER 4
DICK DUTY

"The difference between a dildo and a real penis is that one needs batteries and the other needs leafy greens."

—Margaret Cho

That first session left me shook. I didn't expect a grown man to burst into tears before I'd even touched him. I felt bad for the guy, sure, but mostly, I felt pressure; pressure to fix something I wasn't sure I could fix. I had no real experience, no real answers, and very real imposter syndrome. Still, something about Tom, about all of it, woke something up in me. Purpose activated.

Maybe it was the part of me that needed a new focus. Something to pour myself into that wasn't grief, or my dad, or death. I wasn't ready to hold anyone else's pain, but fixing dicks suddenly felt like my own strange redemption arc.

By nurture and by nature, I was a people pleaser. Thanks, Mom. I was also a rescuer. If someone was in pain, I had to help. The technical term is "codependent." If someone needed me, I felt worthy. I didn't get that feeling much growing up. Thanks, Dad. So this very bizarre job, the awkwardness, the rawness, the vulnerability—I was strangely built for it. I didn't want to just do this job; I wanted to be *amazing* at it.

When I wasn't at The Clinic, I laid in bed, not doom scrolling like a normal grieving millennial, but analyzing anatomy diagrams like I was cramming for the boards. I studied blood flow patterns through the male pelvis, tracking all arteries that served blood to the penis. I memorized pelvic muscle groups. I Googled things like, "taint pressure points," without blinking. My search history was both hilarious and compromising were my phone ever needed for an investigation.

I also had a degree in Exercise Science and Nutrition. I'd spent a decade as a personal trainer. If blood flow was the issue, I could turn these guys into Erection Athletes. I didn't just want to help them; I wanted to rehab them. Thus, Penis Bootcamp was born.

My ideas weren't in the original training in Tucson, but I didn't care. I was improving the protocol. I built educational packets, health plans, lifestyle tweaks, and a whole system to get these dicks back in shape. Shockwave therapy is great, but it isn't a miracle. If your arteries are clogged, your blood sugar is out of control, and you haven't eaten a vegetable since 2009, guess what? Your dick is trying to save your life. Erectile dysfunction isn't just about sex; it's often the first warning sign of a heart attack waiting to happen.

These dicks were waving red flags. I was just the one who had to translate that. So, I gave my clients homework.

First, clean up your lifestyle. Leafy greens. Beets. Omega-3s. Less sugar. Less booze. Less processed trash. More movement. Less sitting. Cardio isn't just for six-packs; it's for dicks too.

Enter the penis pump. Yes, a real device. Yes, shaped like a three-pack tennis ball container. Basically, it's a clear plastic cylinder that creates a vacuum seal around the penis. You pump it like a bicycle pump, but instead of air going into the cylinder, it's sucked out, forcing blood into the penis. And, yes, I had to demonstrate how to use it.

Imagine a powerful businessman with a Rolex, dress socks, and slacks around his ankles, planting his foot on a chair while holding a clear plastic tube over his flaccid penis, trying to look dignified. You haven't seen real vulnerability until you've watched a man suck his own testicle into a vacuum tube while making eye contact with you.

I warned my clients, "You're training it, not inflating a balloon animal. Don't over-pump. Don't forget about your balls."

They never listened. I saw purple dicks. Blue dicks. Sad, sausage-shaped cautionary tales. Every week, someone returned with bruises and lies. And I always knew.

Shockwave therapy, by contrast, was easy. Acoustic waves pulsed into the tissue to stimulate blood flow and break up plaque and scar tissue, like pressure-washing pipes. Some guys felt nothing. Others winced. Some cried.

We offered numbing cream to blunt the snap of the machine. Most remembered to use it. Some didn't. Some pretended they had, then tried to tough it out. Those were my favorite little liars to catch mid-treatment.

Yes, the treatment hurt. I know because I tried the female protocol. Same device. Different anatomy. Let me tell you, it felt like getting snapped by a tiny rubber band for 45 minutes straight. But it worked. I felt like I could pick up a kettlebell with my hoo-hoo (read vagina, but cute). We didn't advertise this part of The Clinic, but the few women I treated left glowing. Literally. Pelvic floor strength for the win.

As I started treating more men, I learned there were all kinds of reasons they showed up. Sure, most were middle-aged guys whose health was in decline, but others were younger and suffered injuries, trauma, stress, or even performance anxiety. Sex injuries? I'm listening. Maybe a little too closely, as my mind went to all sorts of places imagining how exactly that happened. Did they run, jump, or leap into their partner and their dick snapped? Were there acrobatics involved? Toys? Other people? The possibilities were endless.

My youngest client was eighteen. My oldest, 80.

Sherman, the 80-year-old, was a retired engineer with a younger girlfriend in her 60s who, in his words, "Just couldn't get enough." He was charming and unfiltered. After every session, he'd stroll out into the waiting room with his pants half-down, tighty-whities on display.

"Sherman," I'd teased. "You forgot to get dressed again."

"Oh no," He'd wink. "I'm taken. Can't be out there advertising."

He made my day every time. He was vulnerable, hilarious, and deeply motivated to please. He reminded me of my grandma, who was still sleeping with her boyfriend well into her 90s. Legends.

Then there was Benny. Eighteen. Motorcycle accident. Broken penis.

His mother called first, frantic. She couldn't afford the treatments at $500 a session, six sessions required. She begged for a discount. The Clinic eventually caved a little, but not much. Policies were policies, I guessed.

When Benny showed up, he was a terrified, baby-faced kid trying to play it cool. When I met his eyes, he dropped the act.

"This is gonna work, right?" He quivered. "Like... it has to. I've never even had sex."

My heart cracked. This treatment wasn't just cosmetic. It was about identity. Futures. Possibilities. I couldn't promise results, but I promised I'd try everything I could to get him working again.

Scar tissue had a different protocol, and it was much more intense. I swapped in the gold wand head on the shockwave machine for deeper penetration. The pain was worse, but necessary. I warned him. He winced but pushed through it.

And every time Benny came in, I reminded myself: This job was not just about dicks. This was about control. About grief. About proving to myself that I could help, where I had once felt helpless.

Shockwave therapy was a tool. I was the therapist. I was the guide. The coach of broken men, broken hearts, and broken dicks.

Shockwave therapy isn't magic, but it's real. And when paired with real change in lifestyle, movement, and a little humility, it can bring a man back to life.

And maybe, in those rooms, that's exactly what was happening to me, too.

CHAPTER 5
DICK DIARY

"Truth is stranger than fiction. Especially when there's a penis involved."

—Mark Twain, probably

At this point, I was getting good at fixing dicks. Like, really good. But I was also living a double life. I was winning at The Clinic and losing at home, when I was actually home. I was the only one in my relationship employed. And while I needed the distraction, I'd be lying if I said I didn't resent Z for not having an income after he got fired.

I felt like the man of the house. Z cooked, he cleaned, he walked the dogs. Emotionally, I was my dad, and he was my mom. And all I could think was: How the hell did we end up like this after more than five years?

When I wasn't elbow deep in medical lube and strangers' pubes at work, I couldn't stop thinking about my dad. *My dad is dead.* That sentence haunted me. I had to practice saying it out loud. I've always had dark humor, if you couldn't tell, but this daily death rumination was entering uncharted, possibly unhinged territory.

I also couldn't sleep. Every night, I lay awake wondering where my dad's soul went. What did it feel like to die? I was paralyzed by the thought of it, like death was hiding in the corner of my bedroom, waiting for me to look away to claim me.

I had a chip on my shoulder, too. Bitter, even. I was a girl whose dad was taken from her too soon. I'd open myself up at work, present as charming and deeply caring with clients, and then shut down the second I left the building. The Clinic was my fantasy realm. My Matrix blue pill. Real life? That shit sucked.

So, I fed the fantasy. What was supposed to be a part-time gig turned into a full-time, five-day-a-week dick-fixing marathon. And I didn't complain. I needed the money. And frankly, the more time I spent avoiding my feelings, the better.

Sure, I still held onto the fantasy that I'd be whisked away by some dream acting job, but in the meantime, my clinic job made me feel like I mattered. And I really needed to matter.

I started logging my stories in the Notes app on my phone. A dick diary, if you will. Every day after work, I'd jot down bizarre, hilarious, or completely deranged events. For what? I wasn't totally sure. Maybe because humor was my family's coping mechanism. Maybe because we're the type of people who make jokes at funerals. Maybe because I already started to believe my experience might become a TV show one day.

I've heard industry pros say writers need to live interesting lives to have something to say. Well... I was building one hell of a point of view.

There was the guy who was fully erect during treatment and didn't know it. That actually happened a lot. Whether from the numbing cream or just temporary nerve deadening from the machine, some men couldn't feel they were hard. Not ideal for shockwave therapy. The skin tightens, the wand ricochets, and I'm left holding a cock that's too stiff for its own good.

Then there was the ultrasound gel. It always ended up on my face, and sometimes in my eyes. Early into my time at The Clinic, the protocol didn't call for face masks. Yep, this extremely intimate, invasive therapy came with zero PPE recommendations. And I had to hover pretty close to do my job well, like within a foot of the goods. Picture my face, one foot away from balls, dicks, taints, and pubes with nothing between us. My professional control and maturity blended with a sprinkle of fear. One clumsy misstep away from mouth-to-dick contact. My imagination sprinted through the questionable professionalism, the infidelity, and the horror an accident like that would incite. We walked a tight line in those rooms.

Oh, and yes, I had to work the taint. I went all under these guys' balls. The perineum is such a wondrous space between two of the most sensitive areas on a man. But blood flow's blood flow, baby. If circulation upstream from the dick was jammed, you clear the river so blood could return full force to where it belonged to engorge the dick to its maximum genetic capability.

I learned the hard way to avoid the butthole at all costs. One misplaced jolt to the wrong area and these men would jump like I'd tased their soul. I felt awful, even knowing the butthole was the access point to the male G-spot. But this was not the time or place to help strangers find sexual freedom. And that wasn't in my job description either, even if I got pretty good at identifying the men who could use that kind of release.

I can't bypass the pubes conversation here, either. My usual demographic wasn't big on grooming, so there was lots and lots of hair to deal with. Hair longer than I thought possible. We're talking contest-winning pubes. It's an odd feeling to be both impressed and grossed out by the human body at the same time. Even when I was dissecting cadavers in my human physiology classes in college, the hair that remains surprisingly intact on a dead body always made me cringe. My mind wondered why in the evolutionary fuck we needed five long inches of pubic hair. What are we protecting and from whom? What threat to the dick reroutes at the sight of terrifyingly long pubes? Has there been a horror movie made about this? *Attack of the Pubes?* No. Because they ain't protecting shit.

At the site of each mound of hair, I wanted to leave the room immediately. But this was my job dammit. Pubes or not. Forest of hair or not. I was these men's first line of defense against their own failing penis. No protection. Nowhere to go, but through the depths of the coarse, wiry thicket to fix dicks. And so I did, despite the furry obstacles.

Eventually, I started wearing face masks. Not because anyone told me to; I simply needed the thinnest layer of cotton separation for my own safety and sanity. I was rewriting the ethical code of dick handling daily. Dick fixing was the Wild West, and I elected myself Sheriff.

Another entry in my dick diary was the guy who, mid-session, told me about his daughter graduating high school. Very sweet. Except... his fully erect penis was leaking pre-ejaculate all over my gloves. I tried to stay present, really, I did, but I started humming the Spider-Man theme song in my head while watching webs of cum stretch between my fingers.

Never said I was mature.

Then there was the client who tried to hypnotize me. The Mormon pastor who forgot the names of two of his eleven children. The man who asked if I could sculpt his dick into a new shape—and he was dead serious. The poor guy didn't like that his dick was fuller on the base, but thinner up top. Um... I may be an artist, but I am not a magician. Some genetics won't negotiate. Try as I might.

I counseled a man deeply insecure about dirty talk and role-play with his girlfriend. He was in his mid-50's with a ponytail and had that life-long weed aura. He never dated anyone that wanted to role-play or name-call. His girlfriend told him she wanted to role-play as a mermaid and told him to be a sea urchin. You read that right. A literal sea urchin. As if that costume just exists on Amazon.

"I don't know how to act like a sea urchin, man. Come on. She's going to break up with me. I'm not adventurous enough for her." He sounded utterly disappointed in himself. Poor guy.

I also got invited to swinger parties. Yes, more than one, and once by a 75-year-old man, who I'll call Mr. Swinger. At the time, I didn't know swinger parties existed outside the 1970s or the movies. And the fact that Mr. Swinger was attending these parties at his age made me feel like I really hadn't lived or hit my sexual prime. Covered in gold chains and leather skin baked by too many beach parties under the influence, I knew Mr. Swinger had seen some shit. As you can imagine, I had a lot of questions for him about what he taught me is called "The Lifestyle". How did it work? What were the rules? Could you really love more than one person at a time?

Lucky for me, Mr. Swinger was happy to educate me. Turns out there are so many classifications and subcategories of The Lifestyle there are entire Venn diagrams dedicated to helping novices like me comprehend it. I learned so much from Mr. Swinger, he inspired me to write a raunchy rom-com movie about two suburban couples trying their hand at The Lifestyle.

I got flowers and gift cards from other clients. I met wives who hugged me like I was part of their sexual-healing journey—and maybe I was. The value I found in helping heal my clients' pain was intoxicating. Thankfully, only one guy genuinely creeped me out; the only man I worked on who thought sitting up on his elbows to watch me hold his penis was part of the treatment. I wouldn't have minded; except he was enjoying it a little too much. He was not allowed back.

One of my favorite patients was a soft-spoken Pakistani man who didn't want his wife to know he was coming in for treatment. He was ashamed and thought his erectile dysfunction meant he was less of a man. The shame he had was a common sentiment among all my clients, whether they admitted it or not. Over time, the man opened up about his controlling wife and how disconnected he felt from her and his role in the household.

I gave him a little amateur advice about what strong women really want: presence, confidence, leadership. I didn't even know what I was saying, but something about his suffering made me channel the advice of a licensed couple's therapist, as if I'd been there too. Bit of a projection, I will admit.

But the man took my advice. He took his power back and made her feel like he could confidently lead. Boom. She got turned on and he got hard. They had sex. He was glowing. It was a triumph. But I felt like the real victor. I felt like I had my first client success story. I helped him. Maybe not specifically from the treatment, but from the support. A win.

As he lay on the table, beaming with pride about the reconnection to his wife and manhood, a tiny fly started buzzing around his dick.

I stared it down. *Don't you dare land on this man's dick, fly. He's coming off a win. We're not going backward.*

But the fly didn't listen. It landed right where a thin sheen of gel glossed his shaft. The fly's feet hit like suction cups. No. After a moment, the fly tried to pull itself away, body seesawing for leverage, wings flapping hard. *Dammit fly, hurry up. You gotta go dude.* But no matter what the fly tried, he was stuck. Half its sticky little body glued to this lovely man's shiny shaft.

There is no way this scenario had ever happened before in human history. These were the moments in life where I wished someone else was there to witness the insanity. A ghost, an imaginary friend, even an annoying dead relative with unsettled business. But no. Just me, a fly and a dick.

The man never looked down. Thank God. I had to solve this problem for him. And I had a choice to make. *Smash the bug into his dick? Flick it off? Which is less obvious to my client and least painful for the fly? Could I zap it with the machine? Oh, God.*

The fly suffered. I suffered. This man didn't realize an entire saga was taking place on his dick. He kept talking, blissfully unaware and I nodded along, happy for his sex life, sweating for his shaft.

After a few seconds of intense internal debate, I took my thumb and smooshed the fly. I killed it right there on his dick. Then it rolled off onto his balls. *Fuck!*

I flicked the carcass away as delicately as possible, trying not to graze the guy's testicles. They weren't numb so he would've felt it. This one in a billion situation was like defusing a bomb.

Those dick diary entries weren't the only stories happening in The Clinic, of course, but they were the ones I could carry without dropping myself, at least initially. I logged the slapstick, the mishaps, the stray fluids, the flies because laughing kept the floor from giving way. The tender stuff, the ruin underneath? I kept it off the page until I could look it in the eye.

You can thank my dad for my sick and twisted sense of humor. If I had to credit him for anything, it's that. He survived his childhood with jokes, and he passed that survival tool down to his kids. It's the only way I know how to live: find the funny or go insane.

That's how I was coping with his death: skimming the surface, focusing on anything but the pain, pretending the grief didn't exist. Maybe denial. Maybe self-preservation. Either way, it felt like it was working.

And in a way, it was. Inside The Clinic, I was building an incredible collection of dick stories. I was not only seeing more dick than I had ever encountered in my life, but I was talking about sex regularly and getting paid for it.

For some people, my job might have seemed crazy. Other people might have somehow found it cool or privileged. I treated the daily dose of dick like a lifeline. Because it wasn't just my dad that was dead – my sex life was, too. I had no dick at home, and it was killing me.

CHAPTER 6
MY LACK OF DICK

"Sex is like bridge; if you don't have a good partner, you'd better have a good hand."

—Mae West

I should probably tell you about the sex I wasn't having. Yes, you read that right. The number one "dick fixer" in the country, at least according to my boss's latest marketing email, was not having any sex of her own. Not with Z. Not with anyone.

I spent 10 hours a day talking about sex, encouraging men of all ages to drop their shame, normalize their sexual dysfunction, and reclaim their bodies. I'd created a whole movement in my head about normalizing sexual dysfunction. I was these men's cheerleader, their confidante, their high-performance dick coach. And yet... I was in a sexless committed relationship. I could not make this shit up. Let's unpack it.

Z was smart. He was sweet, gentle, and supportive. He cooked, cleaned, and folded laundry without being asked. And when I told him early on that I didn't believe in marriage, he agreed, which made me feel both relieved and seen. I'd clung to that belief most of my adult life, probably because I saw so many people trapped in marriages they didn't really want. My parents were one of them. Their relationship was transactional, resentful, and cold. Two ships flipping each other off in the night. I wasn't trying to reenact that in my own relationship. One Titanic in the family was enough.

Plus, there's a part of me that was always drawn to challenging societal norms. I loathed performative wedding culture; the thousands of dollars spent on one overly filtered day. Why would I sign up for that? It felt... basic. Inauthentic. Like someone else's story.

And yet, underneath my righteous rebellion was a much messier truth: I was viscerally terrified. Every time a long-term partner brought up marriage my body recoiled, revolted and looked for the closest exit.

My brain screamed, "No! No! Get out! Abort!" Maybe it was commitment-phobia. Maybe I was just a Gemini. Or maybe... it was daddy issues. Again. Always.

Anyway, back to sex. Or rather, the lack of it.

Sex had always been a priority for me. It was my love language. My validation. Ironically, my way of connecting and feeling safe with my partner. When it didn't happen, I'd immediately spiral. *He hates me. He doesn't want me. I'm not attractive enough. Something's wrong.* Those thoughts lived rent free in my nervous system.

So yeah, being a full-time dick fixer while sleeping half-naked inches away from my boyfriend's dick that I wasn't getting? Sucked!

When Z and I first got together, the sex was good. Easy. Consistent. We were broke, hungry, and still discovering ourselves. I freelanced and chased creative dreams while he finished grad school. We were young and untethered, and sex was our glue. Okay, not like fireworks, erotic, life-changing sex, but it was steady, and I was in a phase of my life where I needed a "safe guy." A yes man. A "beta male". I despise that term now, but back then it made sense to me. A man who wanted to follow me around and please me like an obedient puppy? That dynamic was new to me, but it felt nice for a change.

Then life started life-ing. Z got more stressed about work, family, and finances. We got a dog, Sam, and a car. Responsibility piled onto our shoulders. And slowly, sex faded into the background. With every missed moment of intimacy, I felt more rejected and more invisible.

Teasing Z about not having sex started as a joke. Then came serious talks where he tried to understand my feelings, but nothing changed. Enough of those cycles and eventually I just sobbed.

I'd sit up in bed, crying. "Is it me? Are you not attracted to me? Are you gay? Should we get your testosterone checked?"

I was ready to hear anything... except he didn't give me anything. Just a confused shoulder shrug. I could see in his eyes that he wasn't sure why we weren't fucking either. He was being honest. Which somehow made all of it worse. His reaction gave me a sense of helplessness that only made me feel more alone.

Late one night, we were in bed, lights off, blinds leaking blades of neon onto our faces. Only here, in this blacked out bedroom, did we tell the truth about us. Like the absence of visibility gave our authenticity courage to show up. And I completely cracked. I pressed the comforter's corner to my eyes to dry the tears that preceded my words. Detergent and salt don't mix. I gripped my chest with the other hand to keep from coming apart. Then I squeezed out, "Every day I wake up, look in the mirror, and see myself getting older and less attractive. I see more wrinkles, more cellulite. And one day I'm going to walk down the street, and no one is going to turn their head. And then what will I be?"

Yeah. That one landed with a thud. Even I heard the record scratch in my own mind.

That moment showed me how much I had unconsciously tied my worth to physical desirability. I was terrified of aging out of relevance, out of beauty, out of being wanted. I even processed these feelings and wrote a pilot script for a series called *Irrelevant* about a woman losing her value in the world as her looks faded. In the opening scene, she stares into a fogged-up bathroom mirror and literally can't see herself. At the end of the episode, she's been left out, overlooked and forgotten so many times that when an automatic sink won't turn on for her at the gym, she snaps and murders someone. Symbolism. Catharsis. The usual.

Back to the irrelevance I faced in my bedroom.

That same night, after too many tears about not having sex, our highly empathetic dog, Sam, got up and left the room. She couldn't handle the emotional smog and chose to sleep on the couch. Even Sam was done with my pain.

Z didn't have a satisfying answer for why intimacy wasn't a priority for him any longer. I think his truth lived somewhere between being emotionally overwhelmed by the demands of life and not knowing how to face it. That and the fact that I was behaving like the man in our dynamic. I'd become the doer. The decision-maker. The breadwinner. The strong one. The one Z needed permission from. It threw off our balance, and I had no idea how to fix it. But I knew I hated how it changed us.

I wanted a man who could throw me against the wall and fuck me like he meant it—and then stick around to cuddle. Z couldn't do either. So we broke up, right? Nope. We stayed. Because that's what codependent people do when their lives are intertwined, and separation would be like dismantling a small company. We shared bills, pets, and routines. It was easier to stay in the haze of routine.

To cope, I'd sneak away to take late-night showers after Z went to bed. I'd lock the door, lay on the bathroom floor, and masturbate. Not because it was sexy, but because it was medicinal. A quick dopamine hit. A pressure release. Proof I still had a body. I didn't drink, do drugs, or even indulge in sweets. Masturbation was always my drug of choice. I pleasured myself to fix my brain chemistry and keep my nervous system from spiraling. My own physical release felt like a safe vice. One that didn't need to involve or hurt anyone else.

One night, I caught myself staring at the bottom of the toilet. The porcelain sheen reflected my silhouette back to me.

I thought, This is pathetic. I'm humping my hand on the floor like a criminal.

As if my need for pleasure was something to feel ashamed of or hide. I felt humiliated that I couldn't ask the person I'd built a life with for the sex I so desperately wanted.

I imagined piss droplets and fecal particles making contact with my face as I drooled into the bathmat. This was my Eat, Pray, Love moment, except way more *Eat, Pray, Masturbate-on-the-bathroom-floor-because-you-can't-ask-your-boyfriend-for-sex.*

By the time I started the dick-fixing job, the intimacy between Z and myself had flatlined. We were roommates with a shared history. He took care of me when I worked 50-hour weeks. I took care of everyone else. I had ten clients a day, five days a week. The long hours on my feet hovering over dicks, managing the complexity of how I moved the heavy machine across delicate pelvic quadrants was brutal, physically, emotionally, and energetically. I'd come home from work, collapse on the couch, and zone out like a trauma nurse after a triple shift.

But I still wanted sex. No, I craved it. My sexual repression roared inside of me. Like shaking a soda can and daring it not to explode, I was fizzing with unspent desire. I'd watched my clients heal and return to their partners with newfound vitality and confidence. I'd helped other people have sex again and I was proud of that. So proud. I just... wasn't part of it. And the wild thing? The treatments were so clinical that I rarely even felt sexual energy for any of my clients. Even if the guys on my treatment table were attractive, I wasn't going to let out my sexual frustration by flirting with them while their broken dicks were in my hand. I was a professional. That is, until my "hot dick" crawled onto my table.

CHAPTER 7
MY HOT DICK

"The male organ of love, when viewed in the abstract, is a thing of rapture and beauty."

—Henry Miller

Yes, we've arrived at the question I get most often: "Were you ever attracted to any of your dicks... I mean, ahem, clients?"

Let's be real. In my experience, both personal and professional, pretty dicks are not always attached to pretty men. Sure, some dicks were undeniably attractive. Most of them not so much. But a few? They looked lab-engineered, or AI rendered, but not the AI that would generate three testicles on a man because it's still learning.

These hyper surreal works of art were smooth and veinless with even tone and texture. They were the chef's kiss of dicks. But out of the 400-plus dicks I met, shook hands with, and tried my absolute best to rehabilitate that year, only two made it genuinely difficult for me to stay fully professional.

About four months in, I had found my groove. My pitch was dialed in, my technique solid, and my bedside manner polished. I could anticipate client questions before they even asked them. I knew the patterns. I knew the concerns. I knew how to comfort patients and adapt myself to various personalities and dick issues. I was ready for almost anything.

Then a gorgeous Roman Gladiator God of a man named Brad waltzed into The Clinic.

Brad was in his late forties. Tall. Muscular. "A whole lotta man," as I liked to say. On paper, nothing about his chart stood out. Just another guy in for shockwave therapy. And then I walked into the room and saw his face. Shit.

I've lived in Los Angeles long enough to grow a high tolerance for beauty. The city swims with the prettiest, hottest people from hometowns across the world. You become numb to all the models, influencers,

AI-looking bots that make you feel like you're living in an Instagram filter you can't turn off. But Brad... there was something else. He had that thing. A shyness. A quiet intensity. He was grounded, knowing he had nothing to prove. And those eyes. You know the kind of confident man I'm talking about. When they smile, it feels like they're winking at your soul. Take all my money, Brad.

After clocking his outrageously perfect face, my eyes snapped to his left hand—the survival reflex women develop to keep from flirting with someone else's husband. Under the fluorescent glare his ring finger was naked, not even a tan line. Shit. My stomach did a little cartwheel. One barrier down. Curiosity up. I never pried into my clients' personal lives, unless invited, but I cataloged everything: the watch, the tidy nails, the way his knuckles loosened when he smiled.

And the gorgeous man on my table that was Brad? He had the audacity to be kind. Disarming. Humble. What a jerk. I felt myself getting flustered, sweating under my gloves. My gloves squeaked. My brain glitched. *You are at work, Kristina. You have a boyfriend. Get your shit together.*

But then I saw his dick. And it was... perfect. Smooth. Solid. Thick. Fuck me.

Brad mostly talked about work. He was behind the scenes in entertainment, because of course he was. This is L.A., after all. I tried to act unimpressed, but I immediately wanted to relate to him about how I was also a producer, swap war stories, and see if we knew mutual people. We definitely didn't. I didn't need to ask. My budgets were $500 or $10K raised from crowdfunding or better put, begging my hometown high school teachers to care about my dreams with a "producer" credit on my movie in exchange for their $25 donation.

Brad and I might have been in the same industry, but we were in very different arenas. He was a professional, corporate, big paycheck earning, celebrity name dropping Hollywood guy. I was a professional dick fixer by day and wannabe filmmaker in my dreams. So, intimidated and turned on, I mostly nodded like a dazed teenager at whatever he talked about. Every time Brad smiled, I wanted to crawl into his lap and write his memoir for him. *Get it together, Kristina. Focus on his dick, not on his face.*

A few sessions in, I realized Brad never talked about dating, sex, or a partner. And my mind filled in the blanks. I fantasized about us. I wondered what it would feel like walking down the street with him. My hot, gentle, giant protector. Brad was so tall and sturdy, I could be a fearless little fairy princess around him. No one would mess with me. Brad had the daddy energy I never had but deeply craved. Oh, how proud I would feel to introduce him to my family and friends. Like his sex appeal would be the supporting evidence that I am, in fact, deserving of good things. Like a big, sexy man named Brad. Oof the way I outsourced my self-worth to the man I wanted to be with. Like my value only counted if it came with broad shoulders and a six-foot frame. Textbook me.

One day, I caught myself actually flirting with Brad. I blurted out something dumb like, "Well no wonder you've been so successful. Look at you." *Ugh. Kill me.* My face flushed instantly, my soul folded in, and I nearly dissolved into drywall as I walked him out. I felt like Baby in Dirty Dancing talking about carrying watermelons. Stupid.

My boss clocked my face and dropped it like a mic, "You know Brad's gay, right?"

FUCKAHHHHHH.

Of course he was. Of course he was gay. And somehow... I loved him more.

After that, I relaxed. I felt nothing but comfort in Brad's presence. I was safe. He was safe. Platonic crush activated. Fantasy disarmed. Unpacking why exactly I needed a Brad could wait. There was no time to deal with my own shit. I had too many dicks to save.

The second guy was different. I'll call him Felix.

If I passed Felix on the street, I might not have looked twice. My type skewed tall, dark and handsome, like Brad. But my dating history? Chaos. I was a classic "she must date personalities over looks" kinda girl. If a guy could challenge me and make me laugh, his looks went out the window. Enter Felix.

Felix was foreign, smooth, and intellectually intoxicating. The kind of man who could discuss forty-six topics in 20 minutes and somehow still leave me wanting more. Each visit, Felix brought a new topic to discuss:

a book, an idea, a story. He talked about philosophy, politics, animals. He loved dogs. He traveled. He listened. Our minds tangoed like our lives depended on it. We elegantly danced from one topic to the next without skipping a beat. We could keep up with each other. There was respect, and ease and compatibility.

Felix was basically the ideal man. The kind of guy you could bring around your friends and family and feel confident he would get along with anyone. He was dynamic and I ate it up like my hormones were holding a flash sale on standards. Felix became the session I looked forward to most every week. I fantasized about him planning an international trip for us, perfectly curated down to the hotel room temperature. He'd order for me at the restaurant, and I'd let him. Not because he was controlling, but because he paid attention to every single detail. He would know what I liked and didn't like. He would be so tuned into my needs and my preferences. Like he was genuinely that invested in pleasing me.

I imagined a crisis and him knowing exactly what to do. I could take the back seat and let him drive. I could be feminine and relax, knowing I had a real leader taking charge. I'd never had a man like that. Someone I could lean on without needing to direct every action. Unlike Z, who even before we stopped having sex would stand there naked and ask me what to do, too afraid to be wrong or let me down to take charge.

But Felix had courage. He wasn't afraid to be wrong. He had the confidence to recover from trying something and failing. I trusted him... and he trusted me. With his dick.

Like many clients, Felix became fully erect the moment I started treatment. And I mean from session one, moment one. Neither of us acknowledged it. It just... was. I never really knew why he came to The Clinic, and maybe I didn't care. Felix seemed to have it all together. He was fit, healthy, and clearly his dick was working just fine with me. What could possibly be wrong with him that he needed his dick fixed?

Then one day, a few sessions in, Felix told me about his wife. He'd never spoken about her before, and I don't even think I knew he was married, or I wouldn't have let my fantasies go so far. Turns out, his wife had a chronic illness that left her in constant pain. There it was.

Felix told me he adored her. That watching her suffer had shifted something in him and made sex difficult. He wanted to want it, but the dynamic had changed. She'd become the patient he cared for. And when they tried to be intimate, his body wouldn't cooperate. He didn't want to hurt her. Felix's ED wasn't a plumbing issue; it was grief shutting his dick down.

More and more, men came to me looking for physical solutions to emotional wounds. I did my best to provide intuitive advice, but eventually, I started vetting sex therapists. I needed to refer them to someone who could dig into the layers I wasn't qualified to peel back.

I wanted these men to feel whole. I'd do what I could on my end to support, comfort, and uplift their spirits (read dicks), but their mental blocks weren't something I could solve.

Not that I'm a recovering codependent people pleaser with a messiah complex (okay, maybe a little), but I really cared. These dicks weren't just dicks to me. They were people with dreams, wounds, fears, and the quiet hope that maybe this weird little clinic held the key to getting their lives back.

Once I heard about Felix's wife, I set my fantasy down and held space instead. Maybe he needed one hour a week where his wife's illness wasn't the elephant in the room shitting on his life at home. Maybe he needed easy topics, the reminder of himself outside of caretaking. Maybe he needed someone to tend to him. Maybe we used each other for that and maybe that was okay.

Something new bloomed in me then. A feeling I had previously reserved only for my toxic ex-boyfriends: Pity. At least that's what I called it at first. I pitied Felix. I pitied most of my clients, not their dicks, their diets of silence. I hated how men were taught to armor up, to swap tenderness for brawn and call it strength. Real strength isn't detachment or whatever bullshit script they were handed at twelve. I pitied the lying, the pretending, the bone-deep loneliness of it. Later I'd rename it: compassion. I wanted to hand them permission to be true.

Pity for these men pulled me out of my own suffering and gifted me the ability to focus on the work. And I was determined to give them all I had. My heart took root in dick fixing. I tapped into every resource I had for them. I felt restless to help not just their dicks, but any part of their lives they would let me touch. I felt like a protective mama bear—these dicks were my cubs. They needed me.

And because I felt needed in The Clinic, my voice with men started to rise, along with safety and confidence. Everything clicked. That is until one of the most famous men in the world walked into my clinic and knocked me straight back to my knees, where my self-worth actually lived.

CHAPTER 8
MY FAMOUS DICK

"Those with Big Dick Energy are usually humble in the sense that they don't always advertise what they possess unless necessary, they prefer to show, rather than tell."

—Katerina Lolita, 5 Signs You Have What Is Known as Big Dick Energy

Since The Clinic was based in L.A., the other question that came up constantly was: "Did you ever work on a celebrity?" The answer? Yes. Will I tell you who? Absolutely not.

But I can tell you what it was like to work on what I now refer to as High Value Dick (HVD). Sounds like a luxury car or a virus. Either way, yeah, let's brand it. I had a serious HVD, and it was great.

One afternoon, my boss came to me with his eyes wide and vibrating with gossip. "We've got a VIP coming in. Late-night appointment. No one can see him. He doesn't want to risk being recognized."

My immediate thought: How very Hollywood. But also, fair. No man, especially one with his face on billboards, wants to be spotted walking into a dick-fixing clinic. I asked who it was, and my boss gave me the legal name. Nothing. Didn't ring a bell. Then he said the guy's stage name. My jaw dropped. Him?! *No fucking way.*

Shit. This wasn't just a celebrity. This was a celebrity with a Capital C. Global brand. Entire Reddit threads dedicated to his alleged anatomy. And now that anatomy was literally going to be in my hands. *Fuck me sideways.*

I tried not to let my inner awkward, chubby 11-year-old who used to get bullied at school and hide in her mom's classroom at recess take over. *Keep it together, Kristina. You're a professional.*

And by this point, I actually was. I was deep into my Dick Era. I had my protocol dialed in. I was the Serena Williams of erectile dysfunction. Fierce, unflinching, swatting down performance anxiety like it was just another weak serve across the net. By this point, I could practically hear the crowd roaring when a client finally scored.

I reminded myself of my developed superpower: adapting to any client's personality. Chatty? I could match. Quiet? I could hold space. Creepy? I could disarm. Meisner acting training and a decade in service industry jobs meant there was no vibe I couldn't meet. Even that of a world-famous High Value Dick. I could do this. I was ready.

So when the night came, I stayed late after work and staged the treatment room like it was going on camera. My eyes fixated on all the flaws of the space: the scuffed baseboards, the crooked light fixture, the nicked laminate. I cleaned like I was hiding evidence. My hands trembled as I meticulously wiped the counters, smoothed fresh medical paper across the treatment table and squared the machine so its wheels lined up like soldiers. I adjusted the volume of the spa-like music to create a safe vibe. I refreshed the essential oil diffuser, lemongrass and lavender on full blast. No way the odor of today's previous dicks would be lingering in the air for this A-lister. I dropped the overhead lights to a soft wash, welcoming and flattering for the space and dicks. I wanted The Clinic to read modern spa, not a dick factory.

My HVD arrived right on time. And holy shit...He was not just famous. He was *hot.* Like better in person, hot. Like my head would've turned all the way around and I would've tripped over my feet if he passed me on the street level of hotness. Worse: he knew it.

The moment he walked in with that swagger and that accent, God help me, I felt my knees threaten to give way. My ankles were shaking in my chunky heels. And I was definitely wet in more than one area of my body.

Get it together. You're not here to fangirl. You're here to do your job.

But, damn, that was asking a lot. I don't know if you've ever met a celebrity and felt like you had to treat them like a non-human person. But because they've done or accomplished something you could never dream of or feel capable of, you kind of shrink your entire energy field into that Wayne's World, "I'm not worthy" shit. So asking me to behave normally and professionally felt like the tallest order.

Thanks to my acting training, a nuclear fear of failure, and a thriving shame complex, I did it. I walked HVD through the dick-fixing process like he was just a regular-ass dude. I gave him the usual spiel. Checked all the boxes.

Before I could come back into my own body and check in if I'd even spoken in English, a slow, knowing, and curious smirk washed over his beautiful face. "How is this your job?"

I scanned his face. Was he serious?

He looked at me expectantly. Oh, shit. This mega star was genuinely asking me. Like he expected me to be some elderly nurse with a smoker's rasp who'd seen too much shit in her life to be phased by broken dicks. But I was young, fit, attractive, and hadn't let dead dicks kill my spirit. He couldn't wrap his head around what I was doing there.

I blushed, feeling my palms sweat and knees buckle. *Did Mr. Billboard just find me interesting? Someone call my mom. Tell her I've made it, baby!*

His childlike curiosity disarmed me. I came back into my body and gave it to him straight. "Honestly, I ask myself that all the time." I played the honest, but playful card to disarm him—my sweet spot. It seemed to work on him, too.

We laughed at the absurdity of our predicament. Comfortable now, he asked more questions. Where did I train? How did I get into this? What was it like working here? I loved his boyish energy. Not performative. Not flirty. Just... human. Endearing even.

I felt so tickled and thrown by his interest in me, I almost forgot why I was there.

His dick, Kristina. You're here to fix his dick. Oh, God. I have to see this gorgeous, uber famous man's dick and not ask for an autograph? God help me.

I ran out of stall tactics. It was time to treat this pricey penis. No more fucking around with pleasantries.

So, I took a covert deep breath, a routine I mastered for every client. Anxious to see what lay beneath, I pulled the sheet back as delicately as someone who's about to shit themselves could. And there it was. The HVD. In. the. Flesh.

I stared. Too long. My lips parted, mouth on its way to full jaw drop. I had to force it closed so he wouldn't notice. Had I been able to peel my eyes away from this HVD for even a second, I am certain I would've seen him throwing a proud smirk my way because his HVD dick was... just so pretty. Not a single thing broken about it. The shape? Like a mold. The color? Perfectly even. And the texture? It's like the source of all creation sent it down with a note that said, "Doubt me again, bitch."

The moment my eyes and his dick acknowledged each other's presence; it sprang to life. Fully erect. Happy to be here? Hopefully. Showing off? Definitely. Or maybe just informing me who the real star in the room was. Yep, it's this dick. No contest.

Um... sir... I don't think you need me. Or that's the fastest I've ever cured someone. Do the Guinness Book people take calls after hours? I feel like I'm owed something here.

Once my HVD clocked his very enthusiastic... situation (yes, it was that big), he laughed and admitted he wasn't there for ED. *Huh?* He didn't have any issue with blood flow. He just heard that shockwave might make him bigger. *Oh, boy.*

Technically, there is some truth to this. Improved blood flow can create a fuller, more robust appearance. But it's not magic. It's not going to turn a banana into a baguette. Still, if he wanted to pay full price for a confidence boost, who was I to argue? Especially since he'd been nothing but respectful.

I couldn't just stand there gawking at this fully engorged HVD, I had to work. So, I puffed up my chest, grabbed that notoriously fart-prone gel bottle and squeezed. Blessed silence. No gassy protest from this bottle. *Whew.*

I channeled my most clinical handy work, rubbed the gel between my gloves until it warmed (because I'm a lady) and smeared it onto his rock-hard famous dick. I lubed up this erect penis on a sexy AF celebrity dude while sensual Lo-fi music echoed in the background. Asking me not to get turned on was like asking a kid to ignore a cookie when Grandma turns her back. The soft-core plot thickened, as did his dick, but I didn't have time to get lost in fantasies. He was fully present, engaged, and making eye contact, not doom scrolling like half my first timers.

I powered up the machine. "Here we go. You ready?"

He nodded like he was about to ride a roller coaster for the first time.

I pressed the metal tip to his very famous, very firm anatomy and

SNAP!

"Damn! That hurts." He flinched.

"I know. I'm sorry." I furrowed my brow, kept working.

"Is it always like this?" Boyish charm melted into boyish fear.

"It's easier when you're not erect," I offered, as gently as possible. I had to.

He laughed, mortified. I laughed, more mortified.

"It's not my fault," he said, hands up. "You're here. There's lube. I'm... a guy."

"Trust me, I get it." He had no idea how much I wanted to neutralize the tension for both of us.

"How do you do this every day?" He groaned, covering his face.

We called out the literal elephant dick in the room and the air loosened. Under the headlines and swagger, he was just another human in a vulnerable position. Okay, with millions of dollars, sure, but he had the right to feel all the conflicting emotions any other guy did on my table. This treatment was never purely transactional, and I liked that he could drop his guard so I could, too.

I worked, we talked, but not about Hollywood or fame, and not about his career. I never let on that I knew who he was. I used his legal name, kept the container tight, made it safe. And for some reason, relating to him like that empowered me. I was proud of the courage I found to overcome the celebrity intimidation factor that wanted to take me down.

He asked about my life. How I managed relationships with a job like this? Was I dating anyone? *Wouldn't you like to know, big fancy famous man!* It didn't feel like he was curious because he was interested in me, more just interested in how I navigated my life with this job. And if he was hitting on me, my mind was so far into imposter syndrome from even speaking to him, I wouldn't have picked up on that even if he'd hit me over the head with it.

I told him I had a boyfriend. And he doesn't fuck me! Can you imagine if I blurted that out? Me and HVD, with his most unfortunately perfect penis, alone at The Clinic after hours.

He followed up, "What does your boyfriend think about you doing this?"

"Good question!" I chuckled.

I got that question often, but I didn't want to make him feel silly for asking. Most men seemed confused, intrigued, or a little terrified imagining themselves sleeping next to the woman who touched dicks all day. I wondered if the wives of male gynecologists got the same questions. Probably not.

But despite the gimmick of dick fixing being something that made people uncomfortable or giggle, most people didn't realize how much I gave to this work. Ten clients a day. Fifty hours a week. My wrists, elbows, and shoulders still haven't forgiven me. I had no energy for a social life. I crashed on the couch every night and I slept through my weekends.

This job was intense. But it mattered to me. Deeply.

And HVD? He treated me like a person. Not a technician. Not a fan. Not a punchline. He made me feel special - chosen, seen, in a way my dad never did. Maybe his fame made the feeling hit harder, like his attention notarized my worth. It felt good to be respected and interesting to someone who has seen so much in the world. It was like I mattered to him, too.

Maybe that was HVD's superpower: making each person feel significant. Maybe we shared that same gift. Or maybe, I felt that way because I'd held his dick in my hand. Either way, we had a great series of sessions chatting about hobbies, interests and, of course, dick fixing. He seemed to be happy with the experience and if it helped his confidence, not that he needed it, I like to think I helped with that, too. And whoever benefited from his improved blood flow, not that he needed it, you're welcome.

I still smile when his name hits the headlines. Every time I pass a billboard and see his face towering over the 405, I'm proud that I treated him like every other client who sat on that table. Even the most famous dicks in the world deserve sensitivity, curiosity, and respect. And it's not like I was a member of one of his hundreds of fan clubs, even if I am now in spirit. But not because of his work, because of his humanness. Okay, and maybe because of his dick—yeah, that was pretty incredible, too. Respectfully, of course.

I needed that confidence boost, even if I didn't realize it. My dad was gone, my relationship was sexless, my acting career was stalled—but here, at least, a world-famous HVD thought I was cool. And that night, walking out into the chilled parking-lot air, I felt taller. More valuable. The HVD had rubbed off on me, as I rubbed lube on him. The newfound importance the experience with HVD gave me carried me into the hardest birthday I'd ever faced.

CHAPTER 9
THE DICK'S BIRTHDAY

"Every man dies twice: once when his heart stops beating, and once when someone stops telling stories about his dick."

—Anonymous

That May should have been my dad's 60th birthday. The one he never made it to.

The first year after a death is a parade of firsts without them. The first birthday, first Thanksgiving, first Christmas, first you-better-ask-dad-but-oh-right-he's-dead. My dad had died the week before Thanksgiving, so my still numb family knocked out the holidays early. But his birthday, which came months later, felt like sand in your teeth. Gross.

My family decided to honor my dad by playing a round of golf together at our local country club—the one where he was king and everyone knew his name. There had been talk of turning the event into a real memorial tournament since we definitely had the interest. My dad was the guy people would turn up to see and spend their whole Saturday on the golf course with. They'd play a shitty game of golf, get drunk, sing in his honor, and try to forget they'd lost their hero. But to plan this tournament? The grief was too fresh, too raw, and my family and I didn't have the emotional stamina for it. So we kept it small: immediate family and a few friends, just enough to feel like we did something.

Z and I drove up to my hometown and stayed with my mom. She was still living in the house she and my dad had been renting for the last decade, but only barely. My mom was about to be evicted from the place my dad had thrived, withered, and died. The eviction notice came in the mail the same week my dad passed away. It felt like a sick joke. The landlord wanted to sell, and while my mom bought herself some time with her tragic story, the clock ticked loud.

My mom couldn't afford to buy, and she didn't have the money to rent a place on her own, especially not with multiple dogs. None of us daughters had enough money or space to house her, which made me feel like I failed her, naturally. I made a commitment to myself that one day I'd be able to take care of my mom the way she'd taken care of us. But I failed.

Fortunately, my sister, Lucy, and her husband found a way to buy a house with a guest unit in the back. They offered it to my mom, but the catch was that she could only keep one of her three dogs. They were large and untrained, and Lucy already had two large dogs. Still, it felt like my mom had lost everything in one crushing season—her husband, her home, her dogs, her health, and her will to live. She looked like she was evaporating. She'd dropped to 98 pounds in her grief. Shame hung off her like a second skin. My mom couldn't save the house. She couldn't save her dogs. She couldn't save my dad.

Visiting home was hard. This was the first time I had been home since he had died. Nearly six months had passed, and everything was still in its place. Dad's entire man cave, or as he referred to it, his "Bob cave" was intact. The walls were lined with golf memorabilia; some he'd won, some he'd collected. Once, I had a friend digitally place his face onto Phil Mickelson at the Masters receiving a green jacket from his favorite player of all time, Tiger Woods. Tiger was also the reason I finally wanted to watch golf with my dad. I had a major crush on him growing up. This digitally altered image hung prominently in his Bob cave.

I spotted my dad's cellphone still plugged in at the bar, screen glowing like a stubborn night-light. My mom hadn't shut it off. She didn't have the courage. It would mean he was really gone. My thumb hovered, tempted to crack the phone open and journey into what my dad cared about in his last few years. But I holstered my impulse. I couldn't bring myself to invade his privacy like that, even if I was still in the dark about who he really was in his private moments, in real life or online.

I walked into my parent's bedroom. My dad's things lined the dresser. His closet still held the golf polos, the two threadbare holiday sweaters he rotated every December, the white and blue New Balance trainers every middle-aged dad sports for too many years, and hats. Lots and lots of hats, stacked like trophies on the shelf, the sun-bleached brims curling from years on the golf course.

My heart broke for my mother, the set dressing of their old life still in place. She was in survival mode, not really ready to let go. I leaned in close to dad's shirts and took a whiff. Beer, cigarettes, sweat, and the Polo cologne he'd worn since before I can remember. The signature Bob blend. It hit like a slap and a hug. For the first time in my life, I was happy to smell that nasty cocktail stench. Fuck.

I lingered in the closet for a long time. The familiar odor made me miss him. Why do scents do that shit to us? One breath and I missed him. I'd spent years dreading both the man and his musk, and still I wished it weren't just a ghost of him on fabric. I would've taken the full blast again, the instant adrenaline spike, ears buzzing, heart sprinting, waiting to hear which version of him those heavy footsteps delivered, just to catch that smell one more time.

My mom was getting close to moving out, the purge of his things loomed. Boxes, Sharpies, and a million tiny verdicts. Keep, donate, toss. It's hard enough deciding the fate of your own stretched-out sweaters during spring cleaning; I didn't want to Konmari my father because he no longer "sparked joy". What if I chucked something loaded with meaning? What if I kept what should've gone.

Did my dad actually care about the iconic 49ers jacket mummified at the back of the closet since the 80's? Did he really love that one white sweater that he put on every Easter, or was it just the only "nice" thing he owned? What about the watch he never fixed, but still guarded like a secret? What about all the miscellaneous notes, golf score cards and keys to nothing in his drawers? We had to assign destinies to all of it. It felt like *Toy Story* for grown-ups, but the toys don't wake up to plead their case.

I asked my mom for one thing: his San Francisco Giants hat. My dad wore the crap out of that thing, The brim was sweat-salted, sun faded, and the logo dinged from years of victory taps. Outside of golf, my dad loved baseball and football. He rooted for the Oakland A's in the 80s when Conseco was playing or for the San Francisco Giants once Barry Bonds came on board. My dad made me love sports. I loved how animated he was watching those games. How invested. He'd make funny noises and create his own cheers for his teams like he was auditioning for a one-man pep band.

I remember when my dad took us to an A's game back in the late 80s. We sat in the nosebleeds, hardly anyone else around us. My dad wore green and yellow, head to toe. He looked so cool. I felt so cool being there with him. It's no wonder my sisters and I threw ourselves into sports. My mom and my dad were both excellent athletes. I wanted to make both of them proud. I played multiple sports my whole life, trying to impress them.

We even had a trophy wall in the house. At first, the wall was his. Trophies from golf and rec league softball lined the shelves. If he played, they won. He was always the best player on the team, something my sisters and I had in common with him once we started playing. We picked up the sport easily, had incredible work ethics, and the grit and determination of kids who had talented parents we were afraid to disappoint. Eventually our sports and competitive dance trophies and ribbons surpassed his winnings. My dad was very proud to share the wall with us. His girls were "studs" just like him.

Our house was a museum of sports: signed footballs, framed pins, tournament photos with exhausted smiles from playing all weekend in the sun. Whether it was from pro teams, my dad's teams, or the teams our family played on, we had it all. And now I had my dad's old Giants hat. Thankfully, my mom agreed I could keep it. I tucked it under my arm like contraband, and felt, for a second like I'd rescued a piece of him I could actually live with.

On this same trip home, I walked into the kitchen and almost buckled. There he was. My dad. On the kitchen buffet cabinet inside a fucking box. Not a metaphor. A box. Cherry wood polished churchy shine, with a fucking tree carved into it with people holding hands around it like a PTA meeting for the dead.

I thought, *whoever made this Hallmark coffin for dust, go fuck yourself. Don't try to sweeten cremains. They're crispy burnt leftovers of a body. No cheesy scenery makes that tender. What kind of people sell these damn things?*

My mind raced and recoiled at the same time, then landed on my mom. Of course it took months for her to pick that out. When he first came home, my dad had arrived in a plastic bag inside a cardboard box because my beautifully indecisive mother couldn't bring herself to make a decision on his "forever home" the week he'd died.

I told her we'd figure it out later. Then later sat on the phone with her scrolling urns together, comparing fonts like we were picking out damn wedding invitations. Maybe I even helped her find this ridiculous box with this stupid scenery. But seeing it in the flesh with his not-flesh inside... I hated every inch of it.

I felt for my mom, I did. But, come on. In the kitchen? Is that really the best place for dad's ashes? Next to cereal bowls? Fuck. But where else was she going to put him when he still haunted every room in the house. His wheelchair lurked by the washing machine. His walker leaned like a drunk against the wall in the guest bathroom. Rogue medical gadgets he resisted but needed remained in this house. My dad hadn't left; he shapeshifted.

I couldn't eat in that kitchen. I'd catch the damn box in my periphery and think: *Morning, dad. Just having some Cheerios. How's it going in there? Is it dark? You cold? Should I light a fucking candle for you like the Facebook grief groups suggest?*

I set my spoon down, appetite gone, and glared at the stupid tree of togetherness etched on the lid. *The fuck, Mom? Get him out of here... please.*

Cremation itself felt morbid to me. We burn a person until there's nothing left to reduce and then display them like a keepsake? My head couldn't compute that my father had been melted down to powder, to the lightest version of himself. It felt creepy. Wrong. I wanted no part of it. If ashes on the mantel bring someone else peace, fine, bless them. But me? I couldn't make peace with a body in a box between the napkin holder and the salt. Nah.

We met the funeral director the week my dad died. Most of the arrangements were made ahead of his passing, years of warning that he was dying will do that. Still there were a hundred tiny decisions left to make. My mom crumbled at the pressure. I did my best to speak for her, Go-Go Gadget eldest daughter project manager mode. I translated grief into checkboxes so no one could take advantage of her while she bled. The funeral home was run by a high school friend and his family, which should have comforted me. It did not. I sat on a floral couch, covered in plastic that smelled like lemon cleaner and old lilies, acutely aware that my dad's body waited in the other room to burn.

The funeral director slid us a catalogue. A glossy, bridal-magazine-thick catalogue. *Okay. What could they be peddling us at this morbid place?*

"For only $399," the copy chirped, "you too can wear your loved one close to your heart." *The fuck?* Pendants, bracelets, even a key chain for ashes. Pages and pages of options, too. *What in the Beetlejuice-by-QVC hell is this? Accessories for ashes?*

My skin crawled. I wanted to punch the funeral director in the face. I wanted to call the morbid magazine people slanging this creepy crap and tell them off for profiting off grief. *How dare you prey on families and try to turn their pain into property? What is this a mall kiosk for sorrow?* I flipped to the back of the catalogue, hell-bent to find their phone number until... My sister, Danny, and Grandma jumped right in and loved the idea. *The fuck?*

Danny and Grandma had zero problems with this proposal. They each wanted to wear my dad's ashes on their bodies like it was just another piece of jewelry. I couldn't understand. Why would I want to strap fragments of my dead father to my body and call it comfort? *Jesus Christ. This feels so wrong.* But then a second thought came: Am I the broken one for not wanting it?

I, not so politely, declined the memorabilia. Fuck this. No souvenirs for me, this isn't Disneyland for the dead. Count me the fuck out. Then we had to pick out the urn. For fuck's sake. My mom, the world-class waffler on emotional choices, now had to choose my dad's final resting place. Would he like it? Would he get mad? He still held power over her, even dead in the other room. 35 years of being told she was wrong had hollowed her out, stripped her confidence, and left her questioning every move she made. I suggested she get the cardboard interim to save money. That idea gutted her, but she agreed.

We went to lunch after the appointment, not that any of us could eat. On the walk back to the car, I looked up and saw smoke drifting from the funeral home chimney. Welp. The check must have cleared.

There my dad went, burning and ghosting into the blue sky. What a sight. It had to be him. How many other dead bodies had arrived there on that day in this small town? None. My dad was their body of the week. Their business for the day. I stood there, watching my father leave through a pipe without any power to stop it. If that wasn't hell, I don't know what is.

CHAPTER 10
THE DICK DIDN'T FALL FAR

"Great dick cannot fix bad character."

—Me, too late in life

Dad's birthday arrived.

My family, Z and I gathered with a few of my dad's closest friends at the local country club, the place he'd ruled for the last 25 years. Sun bounced off cart paths, freshly-cut grass filled the air, ice cold beers cracked open: his kingdom. He'd won so many golf tournaments there since joining in 1989, he became a legend. When my parents could fake being great teammates long enough to play a round together, they'd enter couples' tournaments, and, of course, won a lot of those, too.

Golf was the rite of passage in my family that I skipped. I had touched a club maybe a handful of times since my seventh birthday when my dad gave me a pint-sized set of clubs with hope in his eyes. My dad must have hated that none of his girls took to it. We chased other sports, traded golf clubs for cleats and leotards.

My parents met at a driving range, after all. My dad could've gone pro, and my mom had been the first female caddy on the PGA tour in the early 70s. My great-grandfather built a golf course in north San Diego County. Golf was in our blood and our home. Every Sunday, the TV murmured with hushed commentators and polite applause. My dad recorded the PGA tournaments on VHS tapes and guarded those tapes like Scripture. God help you if you accidentally recorded over the tournaments.

If we wanted time with my dad, golf had to be involved. He'd come home after work, pack a cooler without a word, and vanish to the course until the stars pricked the sky. On lucky evenings, he'd let us ride along for a few holes, cart rattling over bumpy paths, sprinklers misting the rough, the pungent smell of mossy duck ponds. He'd play two balls off the tee, play both until the green and toss us a putter.

I was about ten years old the day he pointed at a fifty-footer on the green and gave me a single, serious nod, his version of affection. I had one shot to impress the man who terrified me. I read the slope, set my feet, and held my breath. I felt my palms sweat around the grip of the club. Easy back and steady through, just like he taught me. The ball tracked like it had a GPS all the way until BOOM, it sank with a soft click.

"Hell yeah, girl! I just bet my husband a hundred bucks you'd make that!" a woman hollered from a nearby patio.

"She's only ten!" my dad shouted back, already whistling one of his famous birdcalls. He could mimic any bird. For a fleeting beat, I was the center of his universe—his star on his turf, with an audience. Lord knows he loved an audience.

He told that story for years.

So there we were on his birthday, at his old course, his kingdom. Only there was no king. Just us, chasing his shadow across the fairways he used to own.

My family and his friends hiked to his favorite hole, now swallowed by neglect. Knee-high weeds licked our shins. Sprinkler heads rusted like bad teeth and half the course lay fenced off for future cul-de-sacs. It felt like the town stopped loving golf the second my dad died.

We climbed onto the old tee box, just weeds and dirt, and took turns sending drives into the wind while stories flew faster. I watched grown men sob over my father, and I didn't know what to do with that. What the fuck were they crying about? That asshole?

Despite my furrowed brow, they carried on about him anyway. How he cranked his Bluetooth speaker so loud the marshals gave up. How his legendary drives rose like rockets. How his jokes landed, and his voice carried. How he sang Lionel Richie, Whitney Houston, The Eagles, Frank Sinatra, and even Beyoncé, at full volume with zero shame. He bent the rules to his will, and they adored him for it. To them, manhood meant volume and victory; say anything, do anything, and be the best at anything. They couldn't outplay him, out-sing him, out-drink or out-smoke him, but they could orbit him and feel more alive by comparison.

I envied them. My dad had meant something real to these men; he'd lit up their lives so much they were in mourning. But for me, the bad always overshadowed the good. Their lives felt emptier without him. Mine felt heavier because of him.

We had dinner at the clubhouse after the round of golf. Same bartender since we were kids, same menu. Paul, my dad's best friend, arrived drunk and glassy-eyed, slurring through their karaoke lore. Most weekends until 4 a.m., the two of them sang their demons away. I used to think it was pathetic. But sometimes, I joined anyway, because as much as I loathed the sight of my dad being drunk in his feelings (or pretending to have them), I still loved singing more. Probably his fault, too. Sigh.

Growing up, we belted Madonna in the kitchen during sleepovers with friends until way past our bedtime. My dad had us dancing on tables while my mom, the fun police, begged us to keep it down. My dad would flip on the neon beer signs the distributors handed him for pushing cases at the store: blue, red, lime-green tubes buzzing like a low-voltage halo. He was king there, too: manager of a Bay Area family grocery chain, shaking hands, stacking pallets, holding court under humming lights.

Those colorful neon beer signs were unlike anything I'd seen inside a home. I thought they only existed in liquor stores or on MTV. As a kid, I thought my dad was cool and hip and young since he liked to sing and dance to R&B and pop music. My childhood friends loved him and still fondly recall those moments we shared with him to this day. He'd even change the lyrics to some songs to make us laugh: "Like a virgin, when your tits beat next to mine."

He was funny. Crass, but razor quick. Wittier than anyone. I owe him that, damn punk.

What I didn't know then: "fun dad" was just "drunk dad" in a party hat. Every weekend. Golf by day, karaoke by night, rinse and repeat. What finally stopped the fun wasn't growth; it was a failing voice and legs that wouldn't cooperate. When the cancer took over and he couldn't swing a club or hold a note, life lost its point.

Sometimes I wish I'd never learned that his sparkle came from a bottle. Knowing stole the shine off my happiest memories. Was he fun, or was the beer doing the heavy lifting?

As I got older, the performance cracked. I stopped singing with him. I clocked the rage as not-normal, the disappearances as not-normal, the nightly drinking as really not-normal.

Then college hit, and my first roommate was best friends with her dad. They did lunch dates. They shopped. I was stunned. Confused. Furious. Jealous.

What do you mean you call your dad for advice? Ew. What would he even say?

My bitter little eighteen-year-old brain didn't get it. I hung out with them anyway, watching the ease between them. He hugged her. Kissed her forehead. She called him "Daddy," and I hated it. I decided she was spoiled or he was weak. Their tenderness felt wrong because my normal wasn't anything like that. So my body filed them under "unsafe." They weren't normal; they were the problem.

You don't realize your family is just one version of normal until you leave home. Then you meet another: no booze fog, no screaming, no slow drip of contempt. A dad who shows up, pays attention, doesn't need a substance to tolerate his kid.

That first year away from home rewired everything. I kept replaying my childhood, asking what he did, what my mom allowed, what I taught myself to endure. If ignorance is bliss, awareness is a bitch.

My first year in college might be when I started grieving the father I never got and fighting to make peace with the one I did.

The weekend before finals, first semester, I almost died in Vegas. Honor-roll rebellion: a quick trip with my nerdy friends to touch sin and be back in time for Scantrons. I'd never seen the Strip before. Neon honey poured over desert black, and the December cold slapped our naive faces. We strutted anyway, eighteen going on invincible.

On the way back to my friend's cousin's place, I rode shotgun in her little Hyundai, more soda can than car, cruising a dim Vegas freeway at about 70 mph. The asphalt hummed, lights raced past us, and then, boom, a refrigerator-sized box materialized in our lane like a magic trick with bad timing. My friend had one year of driving in her wrists; it wasn't enough. She jerked the wheel, the car fishtailed, and we hammered the center divider. Metal screamed. The world cut to black.

While I was out cold, my friends yelled my name and shook my shoulders. The Hyundai crouched crooked and hissing; the air reeked of scorched brakes and burned rubber. Before I even blinked, one of them yanked open my purse, sifted past crumpled receipts and dead lip balm, fished out my brick of a cell, and stabbed at "Mom."

My parents were at the country club Christmas party when the call landed. My mom told my dad, and he didn't say a word. He just bolted. Dress shoes, suit jacket, full sprint. He ran the mile home sobbing and screaming, friends creeping their cars alongside, windows down, begging him to get in. He waved them off and kept running. It was cinematic and unhinged, like someone had spliced an opera into real life.

My mom used that story for years to prove how deeply he loved me, even if he couldn't say it out loud. And yeah, I guess that counts. But I'd have traded the drunk-sprinter hero shot for a few sober phone calls in college. Never once did I get a call from him. Not even a text.

After the accident, I walked away with "just" soft-tissue damage everywhere a neck and back can hold it and years of physical therapy as a souvenir. The wreck healed; the image of my father wailing down a dark street never did.

Back at the birthday dinner, Paul's slurred karaoke memories also brought me straight to the good parts about singing with my dad, the buzz of a cheap speaker, a sticky mic that smelled like beer breath and 90s cologne. The way my dad would celebrate anyone who really went for the high note, even if they didn't have the voice for it. He was the ultimate hype-man.

I loved that feeling: the freedom, the bliss, the blessed ignorance of who my dad really was. But once I understood he used singing to outrun his kids and himself, I couldn't un-know it. In the dark winter months, when he couldn't golf, he mainlined music. Before American Idol, singing was his church; after Idol, it became his entire religion.

The summer before I left to study abroad in Spain, we didn't miss an episode. He rooted for Tamyra Gray; I bet my soul on Kelly Clarkson the second she opened her mouth that she would win (and remain the best of all time to this day). We argued through commercials, rewound runs like refs reviewing a play. By the time I landed in Granada for the finale, it wasn't about the contestants, it was about beating my dad. I sprinted to a hot, humming internet café, elbows sticking to fake wood laminate, clicking through pop-ups until the page finally loaded.

And there it was. Kelly Clarkson.

"I won!"

I cheered to a room of confused Spaniards and one bored barista. It felt good to be right. It felt better to beat him.

Those competition shows set him free from needing a duet partner. He'd watch and rewatch the "shining moments," eyes glassy in the blue glow of his phone. I'd come home for holidays, and he'd shove the screen at me, clips I'd already seen twice, choking up over a nineteen-year-old from Kansas belting a ballad like the rent was due. He could weep for strangers on a stage but barely blink for the people in his kitchen. That disconnect scrambled my brain. How did he have Olympic-level compassion for contestants and crumbs for his own family?

One winter night, during the holidays when I was visiting, I found him in the garage, smoking in exile. The air hung heavy—ash, cold concrete, and so much dust. He didn't notice me. He clicked from clip to clip, mumbling harmonies, wiping his eyes with the back of his hand like a proud stage dad. It was sweet. It was sad. It made me ache for the artist he never let himself be. Then I had to snap out of it. He was still the man who blew our house to pieces with rage. Maybe he was softening in his old age. Maybe I was parenting him while he discovered feelings for the first time. I'd lapped him emotionally years ago; he was still dogpaddling in the shallow end.

Singing was where we said what we couldn't say sober. He'd nudge me toward Celine or Whitney and for three minutes we could meet each other in the melody. Sometimes that was the only language we both understood. Smoke, booze, and a microphone stood between us like bulletproof glass, but the notes got through. We could talk in songs, even if the air always tasted like ash. Every duet wrapped in Marlboro fog and neon buzz. To this day, nothing triggers me like cigarette smoke.

My parents both smoked inside the house my entire childhood. The curtains and wallpaper yellowed, and couch cushions held the stink like a grudge. Breathing felt like punishment. I couldn't crack a window big enough to matter. I was a kid; the air wasn't mine to choose. No control over my environment.

A teacher once pulled me aside in highs school and asked if I smoked. She was in chemo, trying to keep herself alive.

"No, my parents do," I said, heat roaring up my neck.

My teacher looked at me with such pity. This woman was dying, but she pitied me.

When I left home, I swore cigarettes would never be in my house again. Zero tolerance. No friends, no lovers, no one got to own the air I breathed again. And then I dated a charming Brazilian grad student, brought him home, and watched him and my dad bond over a pack. Apparently, I was in my "impress Dad with a smoking older man" era. Yikes.

I made the same hard line with booze. High school gave me drunken blackout nights I barely recognized as my own—desperate to fit in, drinking with the football team, feeling nothing until I felt nothing. Blurry flashes: driving when I shouldn't, waking up in the wrong bed, boys taking what silence didn't consent to. I carried the shame and blamed myself, not the alcoholism braided through both sides of my family.

In college, studying exercise science while watching alcohol hollow out my father sealed it. I chose sober on purpose. That choice was the first cut line between me and my family.

Holidays turned into endurance tests. Beer bottles clinked, laughter ricocheted off the kitchen tile, someone lit a cigarette and the smoke spread like gossip. A couple of my sisters took up smoking; everyone drank. I sat stone-cold sober, present enough to hate it and, if I'm honest, to envy it. Why was drinking the only bridge between people? Why did they need a vice to show up as themselves? I missed the chaos I'd sworn to avoid, even as it made my skin crawl. I was drowning in responsibility I didn't ask for but couldn't put down. With no money and nowhere else to go, I did what oldest daughters do: tolerated. The options were to endure the circus or sit alone in the dark.

My dad's golf buddies folded into the mix—summer BBQs, winter game nights. Some of the newer ones didn't even know who I was when I would visit; they hit on me in front of him like I was a waitress at their table. My dad did nothing. No hand on a shoulder, no "that's my kid," no line in the sand. I felt abandoned all over again.

Eventually, the inappropriate became the atmosphere. I tried to out-joke them, to sling a sharper punchline, thinking if I won the banter I'd win back control. But each laugh cost me a piece of myself. I wasn't managing the room; I was bleeding out in it. No one checked anyone, not my dad, not my mom. Around there, "boys will be boys" wasn't a phrase; it was policy. That was just the way men were. Right?

Whispers about divorce started buzzing through the family phone tree like a hornet's nest. Then a rumor crawled out. One of my sisters, drunk and furious, blurted that my father had slept with someone we knew. My mom went quiet-shattered. Maybe it was shame. Maybe it was the moment her denial finally cracked and the truth of who she'd married walked into the room without knocking. Either way, I did what I always did: moved to protect her.

So I wrote him a letter.

This was pre-therapy, pre-boundaries, pre-"use your I-statements." I sat in front of my large Dell computer in my college apartment and typed out the most painful letter I'd ever written. And I wrote break-up letters for friends like it was my summer job in high school.

I mined my chest for something like compassion and wrote: Dad, if you don't stop drinking and smoking, you'll miss everything—us growing up, our kids, walking your daughters down aisles. You might even get cancer and die. I'd been mainlining health and exercise science classes in college; double-blind, peer-reviewed studies made me brave. Also terrified. Hating him was one thing. Losing him forever was worse. (Foreshadowing, anyone?)

It took every ounce of courage for me to write that letter. I even read it aloud to my sisters and mom before to make sure we were aligned in our mission. I emailed it to my mom. She promised she'd print it and deliver it. She did. He read it.

His response?

"Who the fuck does my daughter think she is? She doesn't get to tell me how to live my life. Fuck her."

My mom relayed his message word for word—no cushioning, no editor's cuts. The sentence hit like a beer bottle cracking on concrete. I'd set my heart on the table for my biological father, the man I feared, despised, and still wanted approval from. And he flicked it into the trash without looking. At that moment, I didn't feel like his daughter. I felt like collateral damage.

So I went silent. Three years. I skipped holidays, birthdays, any event with his shadow in it. I never dialed the house phone. What if he picked up? If I heard his breath, my resolve might crack. I crossed streets, left rooms, and shut down conversations. My protest had choreography.

The only good thing to come out of the letter was that he stopped smoking in the house. You're welcome to everyone who benefited from that. It took a small country's worth of energy to hold that line, but rage is a great generator. I clung to my certainty. I was right, he was wrong. I let that certainty harden into armor. I wanted my power back; the power he'd held over me since I was born.

It was a brutal time in my life. My body kept the score with a vengeance: mystery viruses, odd injuries, pain that found new addresses every week. I lost my father for the first time in those years, and then the universe added a punchline: he developed skin cancer. A spot on his lip returned, he ignored it, it spread to the lymph nodes in his neck, and surgeons carved out a path that left a scar like a chainsaw grin. I could only think, I told you so, and that righteousness tasted like battery acid. I was drunk on it. I hated that version of me, and I couldn't stop sipping.

What finally forced us into the same room? The dickhead turned fifty and my mother threw him a blowout. Over 100 family, friends, everyone he's ever known flew in to attend. And my mother wouldn't even consider letting me skip out.

Fuck. He doesn't deserve me to be there, Mom. Not until he apologizes to me. Why should he get to continue to live his life and be celebrated for breaking his daughter's heart?

But my mother's guilt had better aim than my pride. I went. Of course I did. My nervous system revolted: cold sweats, stomach acid, the whole anticipatory-anxiety parade.

I didn't speak to him at the party. My attendance was the gift. He didn't get conversation on top of it. Fuck that.

I parked myself at an over-decorated table and watched the worship service with my arms crossed. People rolled in pallet-loads, and I mean literal pallets, of Heineken, like beer was his love language and legacy.

Apparently to the people who "knew him best," he stood for two things: beer and golf. Neat.

And of course there was karaoke. So I did the only thing that made sense in a room built on denial: I asked the DJ for "From This Moment" by Shania Twain, the duet we always sang together. Fine. Let's speak in the language he actually understands.

I stood on the dance floor alone as the instrumental opening swelled. Someone handed him a mic, and he sauntered over to me. Motherfucker.

We sang. No speeches, no amends, just melody and a truce threaded between verses. Our eyes did the talking that our mouths refused to try. It was the apology we could survive, the only one we were ever going to get. Just the song. Just the line "I live only for your happiness", written by some songwriting bitches who didn't know they were ghostwriting our ceasefire.

Ten years later, at the 60th-birthday dinner for my dead dad, I tried to do more than just take up a chair. I worked the table like a comic on an off night and told Paul about my dick job. I lobbed jokes the way my dad taught me: defuse, distract, delight. I wasn't touching booze, so humor was my only anesthetic. Fine. Let's talk about dicks.

Paul blinked at me through a scotch haze, his smile sliding around his face like an egg on Teflon. The word "dicks" ricocheted off his skull and fell to the carpet. Instead of the disgust I usually reserved for him, pity rose up like a reflex. Apparently, my options with men were binary: hate them or feel sorry for them.

Paul tipped his glass and let his glossy eyes do that familiar twinkle—sweet, father-ish, half in the bag. He was grieving, too, same playbook as my dad: numb it or drown in it.

Between swallows he managed, "You know your dad loved you the most."

Fuck you, Paul.

"He made me promise him to walk you down the aisle if you ever got married since you're the only one of his daughters who hasn't."

What the fuck, Paul?

Rage flared clean and hot. I was not impressed. Also: livid. One of my biggest fears about marriage was my dad on my arm down the aisle.

Now I was getting the understudy? What had Paul done to "give me away?" He didn't raise me. He didn't build me. He didn't earn the right to hand me to anyone. My mind went wild.

You helped wire my hate for men, Dad. You were a paycheck with a pulse, an inconvenience with car keys. Why would I gift you the aisle and let you break the tape at a race you never ran? Father-daughter dance? Hard pass. And now Paul, trotting in cold from the bench to take your victory lap because you ducked your own mess and tapped out early? No. Fuck you, Dad. And fuck you, Paul.

Sitting there at dinner, watching Paul fish for memories with a slurry of Johnnie Walker Red Label and grief, something wedged under my breastbone and wouldn't budge: my father wasn't just my father. He was every man I'd tried to fix, decode, or outrun. The ones who drank past feeling, who wore charm like body armor, who vanished when it counted and reappeared with karaoke and a grin like that settled the bill.

They were the same men I met every day at The Clinic. Men who wept on my table. Men who apologized with performance—bigger tips, bigger jokes, bigger stories—instead of words. Men who couldn't say "I love you," so they pressed a beer into your palm or shoved a mic toward your mouth and called it connection. And there I was, still bargaining with ghosts: if I listened hard enough, held them gently enough, did my job well enough maybe I'd finally earn what I never got from my dad. An apology. A thank you. One clean ounce of validation.

Looking back, my fury wasn't aimed only at him. It was aimed at the water we were all swimming in, the world that told me to be soft and armored at the same time. The society that made me distrust men while starving to be chosen by them, to build my own safety net and then be shamed for not wanting to fall alone. My dad didn't invent that system. He just embodied it. And for that, I resented him, and, maddeningly, needed him all at once.

Maybe Paul was right. Maybe my dad did love me the most at some moment in a drunken haze, whatever the fuck that means. But love without safety, without consistency, without accountability? That's not love. That's a haunting. And ghosts don't walk you down the aisle.

Paul died three months later.

No shit. Heart attack. Or maybe just a broken heart. Probably both.

Now my dad was dead, and even the surrogate father that my dad had personally selected to cover his absence was gone, too. The whole situation felt like a bad omen or a curse with my name etched on it. The father I'd needed was never going to exist, not in the flesh and not by proxy. Maybe I was never meant to have a dad. Not then. Not ever. I was my own bouncer, my own bodyguard. No man was going to step between me and the world.

And that year, I made a living stepping between men and their shame. Protecting them from the stories that gutted them while I carried my own. Ironic? Yep. Life's hilarious like that.

CHAPTER 11
THE VP OF DICKS

"Being VP is like being the balls...you don't give the orders, but you keep the whole operation standing tall."

—Me, after much reflection

Back at The Clinic, things were taking off. We leased the office space across the hall and moved all treatments for dicks exclusively over there. The shockwave machine screamed like a tiny jackhammer, and we wanted our VIPs' identities protected, so the Botox crowd wouldn't bump into them at reception. This was L.A.; anonymity was a love language. We'd only had one treatment room before, which meant lag time while I stripped paper, disinfected the table, and reset the room. In the new space with two new treatment rooms, I ping-ponged from room to room without a breath. We even hired assistants to keep the rooms stocked and cleaned between clients, so I didn't have to do it myself anymore. I'd finish one guy, scrub up, slap on some new gloves and a fresh face mask, and roll right into my next dick. The Clinic became a dick-fixing factory, and I ran the assembly line.

By then I had the dick-fixing protocol down. I started pitching the add-on treatments we'd brought in. We offered blood panels to check hormone levels, PRP (Platelet Rich Plasma) injections straight into the dick, even stem cell therapies. The idea of these advanced therapies was to increase the rate at which the body would heal itself after our shockwave machine caused the microtrauma. And it worked. We were on the cutting edge of dick doctoring, and I sold anything that could truly help. No snake oil, just science and a steady hand.

Did the add-ons bump up my commission? Yes, thank God. Dogs don't feed themselves premium raw food. Upselling slid into muscle memory: if it would move the needle (and the blood), I offered it.

The Clinic started hosting monthly wellness events and that year, we even sprang for a booth at L.A. Pride. I'd never been to Pride, but I always wanted to go. I decided we needed to make our mark with more than just a folding table and a banner to draw people to The Clinic. I came up with the idea of creating shirts for us to wear that said "DICK FIXER" in bold block lettering on the front, and "Shocking Dicks Back to Life" on the back. Black and White. Loud, but clean. I giggled at the idea, but Pride could handle the boldness.

My second idea was a little more... aggressive? I always loved those wacky, waving inflatable arm-flailing tube men. Like every time I'd seen them, there was this little kid part of me that either wanted to tackle them or dance with them. Pure serotonin with a blower. I felt the same rush for mascots. I lived for the British comedy show *Trigger Happy TV* in college. The show had people dress up in mascot costumes and fight each other in public and they filmed the insane scene in slow motion. Epic. I'm not sure what part of me is broken, but that was comedy gold.

So, I thought about how those tube men would collapse and rise, then collapse again. Tell me that isn't the perfect metaphor. I figured why can't we get a custom inflatable dick for our booth? Well, we could, and we did. I even requested a few white streamers on the tip to, uh, clarify the message.

Finally, we hired sexy male models to stand in front of our booth, shirtless naturally, and pass out flyers. I thought we needed to hit the marketing from all angles. I'd worked in casting before so I knew we'd find mature and spunky models who could sell "medical dignity" and "camp" in the same smile. Once the men realized what business they were promoting, each did the same double take and smirk. Maybe they were too young and full of, um, vitality to relate, but a job is a job.

Our booth hit like a confetti canon. The hot models drew a crowd. The bold shirts became unexpected merch we had to take orders for. The giant blow-up dick became the photo op everyone wanted. We became the talk of the festival that year. I shouted our company pitch over the loud music and glittered air for hours at a time, trying to communicate the significance beyond the spectacle. Between bass drops and whistles, I explained shockwaves and blood flow and why shame strangles desire.

Some folks launched right into their stories with me. You could hear how their sex problems ran their lives. I understood more than they knew. Other people hung back until they heard me normalize dysfunction like I was handing out permission slips. A few women admitted they'd never had an orgasm. At Pride, a place built for radical acceptance, pleasure still felt out of reach for so many. Freedom has its limits when bodies won't cooperate.

By Sunday night I was wrecked. My voice sandpapered, calves screamed, glitter lay in places glitter should not be. But weirdly I felt full. We'd dragged these taboo conversations into the beaming West Hollywood sun. We'd told strangers, over pop hooks and parade sirens, that nothing about their bodies made them broken. The weekend cemented it for me: I wasn't just hawking treatments; I was helping people end their private, punishing struggles. The God-given gift of physical pleasure gets blocked for a million reasons. My job at The Clinic was to help unblock it and torch the shame.

Coming off the high of Pride, the owners pulled me into the office one day and promoted me to Vice President. Of dicks. Yes, the VP of Dicks. The last time I wore that crown was senior year when my best friend and I were voted President and Vice President of the entire student body. Honestly, I probably talked about dicks just as much back then. My Lisa Frank diaries were a graveyard of poorly sketched penises with glitter gel-pen veins. Iconic.

Now I was a grown woman with a title I'd never imagined. Once a hopeful actress; now a professional dick fixer. A different kind of craft, same level of commitment.

But the more valuable I became to The Clinic, to my clients, to this weird new purpose that had chosen me, the more I worried I was abandoning my authentic self. The artist. The storyteller. I loved serving people, but I couldn't shake the feeling that dick triage wasn't my life's work.

So I asked for a sign. Literally. I whispered a prayer to whatever cosmic casting director might be listening. Acting still pulsed under my skin like a dormant fever, but I was too busy gloved up and elbow deep in midlife crises to chase anything real. I knew the dream lived in my bones; my days just didn't look like it.

Then the sign arrived.

A Chinese director I'd worked with years ago messaged me. He was shooting a massive Mandarin-language television series in Las Vegas and needed an American woman to play a cop. Small role, huge production. The catch? I had to look ten years younger than I did five years ago. Cool-cool.

This was the same director who once cast me as the lead in his sci-fi graduate thesis film and followed it up with, "You need to go running. The suit I'm making you is very tight." An honest king.

He wanted to meet the next morning. I was already en route to a friend's film premiere that night. No time for sleep, hydration, or a Hail Mary round of Botox. Perfect.

I didn't even need the paycheck; I needed the booking—proof that my career wasn't just white coats and numbing cream. Proof that I was more than a glorified dick technician.

After a frantic Google search, "how to look twenty-five again with makeup and prayer", I met him at a downtown café. I dressed more detective than desperate actress: leather jacket, clean lines, hair smoothed like I had a badge in my pocket and a moral code. I channeled my best "I don't need this" Big Dick Energy. Hollywood eats BDE for breakfast. Act like you don't care, get the job. Act thirsty, the dream ditched you.

The director launched into a two-hour monologue about how our sci-fi film had rocketed him to fame in China. I smiled, nodded, sipped green tea, and tried not to sweat through my vegan leather. I loved him, truly, but was I visually passing? Younger enough? Fit enough? Enough, enough? If this was a vibe check, my vibe needed concealer before it melted off.

Finally, he paused, scanned my face, and gave a tiny nod.

"You'll work for the part. I will put you in touch with the producers."

Done. I couldn't believe it. The universe slid me exactly what I'd asked for. See? I knew I was still meant to act, not just wrangle dicks and build someone else's dream business. Then reality tapped me on the shoulder: How the hell was I going to do both?

Shit. Time to figure it out.

I floated back into The Clinic high on possibility and shoved logistics to Future Me. Any minute now, the follow-up call would pluck me off dick duty and drop me back into the life I was meant to have. Any day. Any hour. Fine, I'll breathe while I wait.

While I waited, I worked.

One of my new clients was a man in his 50's, we'll call him Gary. Sweetest guy alive. He cried from the pain of the treatment every single session. Not a misty glaze, but full-on, hot tears sliding into his ears on the paper pillow. Then, after one treatment, he came in glowing: "Little Gary's working again." Magic. He was thrilled. So was his new girlfriend—let's call her Sarah.

Gary told me everything about Sarah. Everything. She liked it from behind, got so wet they skipped lube, couldn't keep her hands off him. TMI, Gary, but if a man can't talk about his sex life while his broken dick sits in a stranger's gloved hand, when can he? They were both divorced, rediscovering sex like teenagers with a Costco-sized box of condoms. I knew so much about their bedroom life I half-expected a SAG credit.

One day, Sarah came in with him to The Clinic. Oh, shit. The other woman. Well, the first woman, but in Gary's dick's life, I was definitely the side piece.

Was she here to hate me? To watch and judge? To challenge me to a duel with ultrasound wands?

Sarah took one look at me and wrapped me in a hug like I'd handed her a second life. Hug? Not on my bingo card. If caramel apples were a person, they'd be Sarah. Her energy was shiny, warm, a little sticky sweet. She and Gary had that fun, permissive energy of the parents who let teens drink at their house, as long as everyone surrendered car keys and slept on the couch. They were adorable. The love between them felt easy, fizzy. I was weirdly honored to witness it.

Then she asked to watch the treatment.

"Um...?"

I glanced at Gary who was on board before I could respond.

They grinned like two little kids in a candy store.

"So this is where the magic happens?" she chirped, peering around the room.

"I guess you could say that." If she only knew how un-magical most men felt in here.

Sarah settled into the corner chair, radiating bubble-bath warmth, and chatted the entire time I held her boyfriend's dick in my gel-slick gloves. The diffuser pushed out orange blossom essential oils, the machine hummed like a muted jackhammer, and I realized I'd never had an audience before. I'd certainly never held a man's penis while someone else observed from the splash zone. My sex life was aggressively vanilla—voyeurism and threesomes had not RSVP'd to my bedroom. I worked hard to make this room private and sacred. I had not anticipated spectators.

And yet there we were: me, Gary, and Sarah, two lovers and their very involved dick fixer, doing our best to make a little more magic.

According to Sarah, I was the unicorn in their sex story. I'd learned that term from another client, poly folks call the single woman who joins a couple a unicorn. In their little fantasy, I'd become the nurse-unicorn with a name badge and nitrile gloves, which I did not want to be. But they were so wildly in love, and their sex life was finally thriving that when she asked to observe, I couldn't say no.

Then Gary upped the stakes. He'd bought Sarah a treatment of her own and wanted to do it that day.

Is that why she is here? Oh, my.

Yep, the female protocol. I'd tried it on myself and done it once on someone else. Fixing dicks? Easy. At this point I was immune to dicks in general. I'd held every variety: shapes, sizes, shades, scents. A penis is an external organ; point and shoot. A clitoris? Some labia I'd never seen before? A vagina is the eighth wonder of the world. More nerve endings, more nuance, more... responsibility.

Suddenly the room felt intimate in a different register. I wasn't just supporting a man's sexual function; I was helping a woman fine-tune hers. Still clinical, but the threesome energy in here slid from "mystical unicorn saves the day" to "two girls playing My Little Pony while Dad supervises," which, let's be honest, was weird.

When it was Sarah's turn, she giggled, winced, and squeezed my forearm as the machine snapped. Cool gel. Warm diffuser air. The wand's staccato tap-tap-tap. I was terrified I was doing it wrong, and of course I acted like it was just another Tuesday. No one wants to learn they're the guinea pig for a medical procedure. Frankly, no one wants to be the fifth pig, either. You don't mess with the clit. It's got enough problems.

Sarah was a champ. We breathed through each pass, and we got it done. Apparently, it leveled them up... again. Gary arrived at his next session with a full play-by-play. Extremely specific, too. I learned exactly where they buy their sex toys and that Rodrigo always gives them the senior discount. Turns out vibrators and anal beads in your 50's come with perks, even in L.A. Sarah sent her regards.

At the end of his package, Gary sent flowers. "You changed my life," his note said. The bouquet was gorgeous. I felt like a proud mom at graduation: caps, gowns, erections. Sweet Gary and Sarah had no idea how much pleasure... okay, poor word choice... eh hem, joy I got from working with them. I didn't know couples in their 50's could be that connected and that horny. It gave me hope... and it made me ache. Where was that kind of passion in my life? I wanted it badly. For now, at least I got to witness it. Proof the spark can survive and that joy and freedom are accessible, at any age.

The next guy I treated? Not the same vibe.

Enter Jack. Mid-40s, married, two young kids. He strutted in like a mall peacock with his collar popped, wristwatch flashing, cologne arriving a full minute before he did. Not demure. Not mindful. I've gotten good at spotting insecurity dressed up as swagger, and Jack was all feathers and no flight.

He opened with a monologue. "Our open marriage is amazing. She sees other people. I do too. It's great. I'm living a literal fantasy."

Okay, bro. My name is Kristina. I'll be treating you today.

That was within the first few minutes, before he'd even sat on the crinkly paper. The delivery felt... practiced. Like he'd workshopped the sales pitch in the mirror. Too quick, Jack.

I stayed curious. "When's the last time you hooked up with someone?"

He blinked. "Oh, uh... you know. I don't kiss and tell."

Uh-huh. His eyes darted to the floor; his wedding band clicked against his phone; his knee started a nervous drum solo. You know that textbook male anxiety twitch, the knee trying to run while the mouth lies. Classic.

I didn't buy it. Something was off. And maybe I was projecting. Maybe the idea that you could love one person and still have sanctioned sex with others made some hungry, restless part of me sit up. Maybe I was jealous. But the way he sold it—loud, boastful, like a timeshare pitch for his libido—rang false. My suspicion stuck like the fly to my Pakistani client's shaft.

That's how the next few sessions went: Jack posturing, me probing. He'd swagger in, bragging about how blissful his marriage was; I'd tilt my head and ask how it actually worked. I'd never met anyone in an open marriage. Open relationships, sure, but vows plus variety? That was new. The whole concept tugged at me. Dangerous. Taboo. I wanted the blueprint. Who pulls this off without detonating the house? Do they have some secret setting the rest of us don't? Like an upgrade in how they see love, partnership, even sex? Could that be me? Would opening the door solve the stalemate with Z, or just invite in a tornado?

Remember, I was elbows-deep in writing a raunchy rom com about swingers. Yes, different lane. Swinging is a team sport; an open marriage is solo missions. Still, research was research. So I listened.

It took a few rounds of Jack's strut and maybe the slow realization that I was a safe vault before he let the air out of the story. Between boasts, he'd glance up and say things like, "You're too attractive to be a dick fixer... maybe that's your secret weapon for healing men." He'd raise his eyebrows, like he'd been the first to point that out. Or maybe I'd take the bait and be one of his new girls. If he was hitting on me, his hypothesis was DOA.

You're not my type, Jack, and also... the way you've been oversharing, I can tell there's some hurt and trauma and brokenness—and I'm not here to fix that for you or add to it. I see right through you, Jack. You're not fooling me, bro.

And then he cracked. The jaw unclenched, the shoulders dropped, his wedding band started doing nervous laps around his finger.

"My wife, Veronica, she's... in a relationship." He squeezed out.

Oh?

"Not just sex. A whole-ass relationship." He swallowed. "I've never been with anyone but her."

Damn.

Tears brimmed. "It's fine, though. She always comes home."

That line sounded like a sedative he'd prescribed himself.

I softened. "Did you want an open marriage?"

"...No. She did."

I wanted to shake him. Of course his dick didn't work. How could it, with his heart white-knuckling the emergency brake?

At first, his arrogance repelled me. That's my usual response to peacocking: the bragging, the posture, the performative chest. Loud cars, small dicks – day-one folklore. Men who broadcast that hard are usually compensating and it's a massive turnoff for me (and every woman I know).

But now, with Jack's broken dick in my expert hand and tears slicking his lashes, I just felt sorry for him. Fuck. Fuck me. The jackass armor slid off, and the overlooked little boy peeked through. Under the pride: heartbreak, deep sorrow, a hot blush of shame. That was the real Jack, the one who'd shown up here. He wanted proof he wasn't defective. He needed to hear he was still a man, still a worthy husband and father. That his body could work, even if his life had come apart.

My chest pinched for him. I slowed the wand, let the machine's hum fade, and offered what I had: space, steadiness, a box of tissues I cracked open like a peace offering. I listened and let the silence do the heavy lifting, nodding as he spiraled through every fear. I shelved my opinions. Tucson hadn't trained me for this; there's no protocol for the kind of dick you fix through grief.

"I have a sex therapist friend. I think you should call her." I said finally.

At that point, I'd practically put through escrow on a beach house with all my referrals to this woman. I could help the physiology; I couldn't untangle the psychology. Jack needed someone to walk him through the bruise of his wife's affair, layer by tender layer. That's not my degree. Thank God for the army of sex therapists in L.A.

Jack agreed. A week later, he canceled the rest of his sessions with me. He'd already paid and didn't ask for a refund.

"I need to focus on saving my marriage," he pleaded over the phone.

My stomach dropped like an elevator. Powerless. The fixer in me stood there with clean gloves and nowhere to put my hands.

At home, Z and I kept slipping. All day I sent other people to sex therapy; at night I stared at our ceiling fan and wondered if we should be in those chairs, too.

I pitched it gently. "Let's see a sex therapist, carve out time to work on the part of us that's gone missing?"

Maybe he could get his hormones checked. Some of my guys had testosterone so low it might as well have been on airplane mode. Maybe that was it. I was desperate to diagnose our invisible sex life; my brain doesn't rest until it finds a fix.

Z never flat-out said no. He nodded, rubbed his jaw, said, "Yeah, that makes sense," and then... didn't call. If Z didn't want something, he starved it with silence. Avoidance? Sure. Fear? Absolutely.

It wasn't just sex stuff. Anything that required internal heavy lifting got the same treatment. We even set New Year goals... me pumping his tires, praising his ridiculous brain, promising him his mojo was in there somewhere if he'd just grab it. Blah, blah, fucking blah. Nothing changed. He chose small and safe.

And here's my part: I kept loving his potential, not the person in front of me. Classic me. I fell for the projection, then sulked when the real man didn't evolve into my TED Talk about him.

With Z, inaction became a flex. His quiet lack of control over anything made him squirm, like telling a stranger why he wouldn't sleep with the girlfriend who fixed dicks for a living.

We stayed at an impasse, sad and sexless, until Z's phone outed him. Texts to a younger girl from our gym. And the cherry on top? I learned he'd been sneaking weed with his buddies behind my back. I'd been sober nearly two decades; I didn't get the vice, and I really didn't get hiding it.

I'm not a phone snooper. That's high school shit. If you need to scroll your partner's messages, trust has already left the chat, and you'll always "find" what you're looking for. Confirmation bias 101.

But this time he left his phone unlocked on the counter while I ate. The screen lit up and a name, Chloe, floated across the banner. Odd. Why was she texting him? This was before you could hide previews. Thanks, Apple.

Every hair on my neck lifted. My spoon froze mid-air. My face flushed as my ears started to ring. Intuition yanked the fire alarm; my body went full DEFCON 1 before my brain could vote. I was shaking, heart punching my ribs, the kitchen narrowing like someone cinched a hoodie around my face. And I read.

And there it was right on the lock screen. Flirty pings about "planning an orgy" and "sparking up together." I didn't even need to scroll. Fresh. Active. The most recent thread on the phone of the man I'd lived with for six years. What in the actual fuck.

For context: Z was a daily pothead before we dated. He knew I couldn't stand smoking, so he quit, unprompted. Same story I'd seen before. Men clock my sobriety and announce, "I'll stop out of respect," like they're pinning a medal on my chest. Then, months later, the "respect" curdles into secrecy and resentment, as if my existence padlocks their pleasure. I never asked anyone to be sober with me. Still, I kept getting cast as the warden. Betrayal after betrayal. It made me nauseous, like I was the reason they couldn't breathe.

So there I was at the kitchen counter, both hands flat on the cool marble, trying to corral my nervous system into anything but a scream. The rage monster I tucked into bed in my twenties, after I stopped trying to fix my dad, kicked the door down and strolled in like she paid the rent.

My jaw clicked shut. Breath shallow. Skin on fire. I could hear my pulse in my ears as the facts rearranged themselves into a story I did not want:

Is this why he won't fuck me? Is he cheating? Having fucking orgies? Seriously? Did he really think I wouldn't find out? Is she prettier than me? She's younger. Is that really what this is? I'm only 35, but somehow, I've aged out of my prime. Fuck. I'm already a statistic. It's a tale as old as time: your man leaves you for a younger woman. Damn, I thought Z had more integrity than that. He can't do better than me. I dated down to be with him. He's a beta male. He's a doormat. He can't just fuck around. This isn't how this works. I'm in control here.

Yeah, I didn't say my thoughts were great or kind. And I certainly wasn't in control—or we'd have been having sex.

I shot up from my chair with Z's phone in my hand and confronted him in the bedroom. His face drained like someone yanked the plug on his bloodstream. He snatched the phone back, thumbs flying, and poof, the thread vanished. Then he stared at his phone full of shame, knowing he fucked up. I tried my best not to break something. That wasn't my style. I didn't want to scare my dogs. I wanted him to read the text back to me and explain himself. But, instead, he mumbled the line every coward rehearsed: "What text?"

Fucker.

Convenient. Immature. Fucking stupid. I felt sick. But did I leave? Of course not.

Miserable as I was, I was loyal and dug in. I didn't know how to dismantle our life—split the bills, the dogs, the history—so I clung to the one thing I could grab: control. He'd lied. He'd betrayed me. Now he owed me. He had to fix it.

So I dragged him to therapy. I found a couples' therapist. I made the call. I even upgraded us to the horse version. Equine therapy? Shit, if we were going to sift through our sexual apocalypse, I wanted to do it outdoors with something that smelled like hay and honesty. Horses don't text randos about orgies when they're not sleeping with their girlfriends.

And equine therapy was legit. We stood in a sun-bleached arena that reeked of dust and horse shit while a giant stallion flicked an ear and read our nervous systems like subtitles. Horses give real-time feedback on your energy: congruent, they soften; chaotic, they move away. The therapist handed Z the lead rope. He clucked, tugged, postured... nothing. That horse was planted like a sofa. Our dynamic, in 1,200 pounds of mirror: Z couldn't move it an inch.

I took a step toward the horse to save Z from the embarrassment of failing his first test with the therapist.

"Don't enable him." The therapist clapped at me.

Fuck. I'm my mom. Always rescuing. Always controlling. Great. You take cash or card?

When it was my turn, the horse clocked me once and fell in step like we'd rehearsed it. Lead rope slack. Hoofbeats syncing with my breath. Of course he did. Animals smell hierarchy and heartbreak. I was a leader. A protector. A self-reliant woman performing the role of the man I'd always needed. I'd never gotten to be the little girl who follows, not with my dad, not with exes, not with Z. I initiated. I lifted. I carried. No one was coming to save me, and even the horse read that off my bitter, but desperate skin.

A few weeks later at The Clinic, Jack reappeared, a surprise appointment, but this time with his wife, Veronica. *Gulp.*

They floated in wearing matching smiles that squeaked like new shoes. Too bright, too tight and polished for public consumption. I felt my spine stiffen into HR-approved warmth. I knew too much: the tears on my table, the panic under Jack's peacocking, his longing. I hated his sad truth and even more that I knew about it. Their couple's grin bounced off me like sun on glass.

Be professional, not protective, Kristina. I had to convince myself that I didn't know the whole story. Her side.

I steadied my voice, offered water, and gestured to chairs. Still, immediately, I didn't like her. Historically, I always defaulted to Team Woman; men were the hazard, women the collateral damage. But The Clinic had scrambled my wiring. Day after day I'd watched men cry into their knuckles, apologize with their whole bodies, grief pooling where bravado used to be. I'd learned men can hurt the way we do. And women can hurt men, with the same precision. The playing field wasn't level; it was a funhouse, every mirror true from a different angle.

I knew I had to rewrite my whole script. Men and women weren't opposing teams, just rotating heroes and villains. And right now, the villain wore mascara, and the victim slapped his phony peacocking grin right back on like it never left. I had no clue how to play it.

Jack said he was there to use one of his sessions and wanted Veronica to see what he'd been doing. Then he added he wanted to gift one of his sessions... to her. Fuck.

I had to treat her? The villain. The woman who made you cry last time I saw you. What is this bullshit? Come on, Jack. You can't expect me to forget about that. You were so fucked up last time we spoke; you canceled all your remaining sessions. What is really happening here and what am I being pulled deeper into?

Ever the professional, and with no real out, I agreed to the double. We filed into the room: Jack, Veronica, and me. The hero, the villain, and the unicorn. Okay, more like the chained-up dragon in the basement.

Jack stretched out on the table, the air heavy with his previous confessions. Veronica claimed the single vinyl chair; legs crossed at militant angles. I snapped on gloves, checked the wand, pretended this was standard operating procedure: just me, handling a heartbroken husband's dick while his wife observed. I made small talk, asked soft questions, tried to read her tells: the tight smile, the stiff posture, the way her eyes never looked up from her phone. I matched the room's hum, professional and pleasant, like this was the most normal threesome a clinic had ever hosted.

During the session, Jack kept trying to get Veronica's attention. "Babe, watch this! See, it's just like I told you. I was telling her all about you, Kristina. Wasn't I babe?"

Veronica didn't bite. She sat very still; eyes fixed on something far more intriguing on her phone. She was elsewhere. Anywhere but there.

Her indifference was surgical and familiar. I'd seen that exact glaze on my mom's face while my dad belted Lionel or recapped eighteen holes of golf like the back nine was a hostage situation. My mom wanted nothing to do with his joy or his escape. Years of being deprioritized had sanded her down; dignity, pride, and her own spark filed to nubs. Connecting over what lit him up? She couldn't. Not with the clubhouse bar bill his absences had left her to pay.

In that chair, Veronica became my mother: cold, detached, checked out. But hold up—my mom was the hero and my dad the villain. Why did it feel flipped in this room with two people I barely knew? Because I only had Jack's side. Wait, I only ever had my mom's side, too.

A hairline crack zipped across my narrative like a mirror dropped on tile. Maybe my dad wasn't only escaping us; maybe he was starving for someone to see him. Maybe he didn't have the tools to ask for what he needed. Oh, fuck me, were those sloppy, drunken performances just clumsy prayers for connection? Attention. Approval. A please-love-me sung at full volume because speaking it felt impossible.

It broke me watching Jack chase his wife's validation and get nothing back. The scene hit a bruise I knew by heart.

Dad, look! See? Am I worthy now? Will you be there for me now? Will you stick around and be a safe place for us?

The horrid truth slid in anyway: my dad had begged for validation, too. Maybe from my mom, maybe from all of us. For one queasy second, I saw the little boy inside him, the same boy blinking through Jack's swagger. The same kid I carry. Fuck.

I hated that glimpse. Hated that forgiveness even knocked. The idea that my dad might deserve permission to be flawed scrambled my insides.

Fuck you, Jack and Veronica. How dare you humanize my father.

Then it was Veronica's turn. Of course it was. I'm sure Jack gifted her a session thinking it would superglue their marriage back together. His tone gave him away: familiar, salesman-bright, the exact pitch I've used to sell my own worth.

"See? Isn't it great? Just like I said. I knew you would love Kristina."

The lesson kept walloping me. Jack wasn't a peacock; he was a boy tugging Mommy's sleeve for a gold star. Their dynamic mirrored me in high school: honor roll, MVP, VP of the whole school, scholarship grave robber, performing excellence like a hostage trade for attention.

Look, Dad. Am I enough now?

My dad had been that boy, too: winning everything, building armor out of trophies because his own parents never showed up to clap. Jack threw money at the hole in his chest. I hurled work ethic at mine. My dad poured beer into his.

Back in the room, Veronica lay down, legs open, chin tilted, thumbs flying across her phone like she'd booked a manicure, not a clitoral shockwave. The piercing sound of the machine punched through the air but missed her. She was too busy texting her boyfriend, or at least that's where my imagination went. The treatment was not the wake up call she needed. My stomach flipped. I pictured the "results" of this session earmarked for her next lover, not Jack.

A mean part of me wanted to dial the settings up on the machine. A little extra pop to snap her into the reality of her husband's needs. I didn't. Of course I didn't. My moral compass, and, fine, the imaginary HR manual we never had, held the line. We were operating in the Wild West of sexual dysfunction; half the "protocol" was invented in hallways. But still.

Worse, another part of me almost understood her. Maybe she didn't respect Jack. Maybe she was stuck with him. He's the father of her kids. My mom was the mother of my dad's. People stay for money, for mortgages, for the choreography of being known. They stay married to the Peter Pan man-boy who refuses to grow up.

That night, after Jack and Veronica left, I couldn't shake the image of Jack's face when he looked at her. The pleading. The quiet desperation. The flicker that whispered maybe this would finally fix it all. His misunderstood SOS felt too much like my dad's. I'd always decided he chose golf and beer and karaoke over us. Maybe he couldn't choose us. Maybe no one had ever chosen him. Maybe you can't hand out what you never got.

I'd spent years convinced men were either dangerous or indifferent, too armored to offer the softness women needed. Some were soft, but many men were just boys with beards, buried in shame and silence, hoping someone would meet their eyes and say, "I see you. You're enough." That's all I ever wanted to hear. It's probably all my dad wanted. Maybe Jack. Maybe even Z.

Peeling back the layers of male shame pissed me off and moved me in the same breath. Grace felt like a coupon I kept handing out while I was still paying full price. Where did mercy end and accountability begin? Maybe that's why I was the VP of Dicks, not the CEO: I could restore blood flow, but I couldn't rewrite a childhood. Latex helps with fluids, not feelings.

So I focused on the levers I actually could control: gloves, settings, boundaries, my voice. If I couldn't fix the whole man, I could stop confusing compassion with permission. I could learn where repair ends, and self-respect begins.

The mystery of men wasn't a problem to solve; it was a tunnel that kept curving.

Fine. I'll bring a flashlight, not a sledgehammer.

INTERLUDE
THE LONG DICK DRIVE

"Life-or-death decisions are just like dicks...
it's all about timing, pressure, and knowing when to let go."

—Someone, I'm sure

The day we drove north to say goodbye to my dad finally showed up like a summons.

My grandmother rattled up from San Diego on the train and met us in L.A. Z and I rented an SUV because our sedan couldn't swallow two dogs, my grandma, suitcases, and the refugee camp of perishables I refused to let rot. Death turns you into a project manager: you inventory grief, label it, and pack it in a cooler.

Z took the wheel. Grandma claimed shotgun. I wedged myself in back with the dogs, their nails ticking the plastic cargo mat, the air a mix of dog breath and citrus cleaner. The I-5 stretched ahead, one long gray sentence I'd driven a hundred times, but never to hold my father's hand once more and then let it go.

If we're lucky, we get to say goodbye to our parents. No one tells you the goodbye begins three hundred miles out with a full tank of gas and a pit in your throat.

By late afternoon, the light went honey thick. The Central Valley of California's hills rose and folded like the backs of sleeping lions, and the grasses burned that exact color my grandmother lived to brag about. For the four-hundredth time, she offered her TED Talk: "It's the Golden State because of these hills, not the Gold Rush or the sunshine." She'd been in California her whole life and treated its trivia like a family recipe, repeat as needed, serve warm. I watched the slopes glow, nodded like a good audience, and let the facts briefly push the fear aside.

I let her talk. My grandma's oldest son was dying. Earlier that year her stepson, my uncle, had died by suicide. The year before, her grandson, my cousin, was gone at thirty-five. Judgment didn't get a seat in this car. Only loss did. Only support.

My phone wouldn't stop twitching in the cup holder: texts, missed calls, voicemails piling up like taillights on the Grapevine. Where are you? How close? How much time? Their urgency needled my ribs, but I knew it for what it was: the only lever left when everything else slips—ask for an ETA and pretend the clock listens.

Then the call I didn't expect lit up my cell: Ethan.

My brother-in-law, Ethan. The strongest, most alpha male in our family. He packed broad shoulders, a low golf handicap, and was the rare man who could play eighteen holes with my dad and never blink. Because he refused to be intimidated, my dad adored him. They'd grown tight at the end.

Ethan may have been the only person in our family strong enough to say the words out loud to me. He swallowed once, twice, then forced out the words, his voice arriving sandpapered and thin.

"Kris," he said. Ethan and Lucy called me that. "They're losing him."

"What do you mean?"

"It's happening. His lungs are filling up. He's choking. They can't stop it. There's only one option left and it's not what he wanted."

Cold washed right through me. This was TV-script stuff, not my life. Not my father.

But the last few years already played like a horror reel. A spinal tumor folded him like a backward hinge. Before the surgeons took him in to bolt in two gleaming rods into his spine, in pure Bob fashion, he demanded a cigarette. Nurses declined, so Ethan stole a wheelchair from an empty room and snuck him out to the parking lot, IV bag still attached, to join my mom and Lucy, so he could inhale a pack of Marbs and smoke and crush a sleeve of Double-Stuf OREOS. Protocol was for other people; nicotine and chocolate weren't. Not for my dad.

Later he fell down hard and couldn't get up. Not a cute Life Alert gag; a mid-50s man bellowing for my mom because the muscle had melted off him. No button around his neck. No cavalry. She couldn't lift dead weight, so she'd call my sisters, or one of his golf buddies, to come hoist him like a ruined sofa. Radiation had blistered his back; grab him wrong and his skin would shear, hot and glossy, like the lacquer on a rotisserie chicken.

The bedsores tunneled so deep into his flesh you could see anatomy textbooks in real time, skin, fat, muscle and eventually the bright, horrifying gleam of bone. Cysts colonized his face for reasons no one could explain. My sister Lily, both a saint and a lunatic, learned to lance them. Sometimes the timing betrayed her, and they burst across her cheek. She said the smell was death itself, and I believed her.

Forty-something pills a day loosened his teeth until they surrendered, except the tooth fairy doesn't come to death's door. Diapers replaced briefs. Showers turned into wipe-downs. Near the end he needed oxygen just to sip air. He became a gasping outline of himself; more exhale than man. A nightmare that refused to end. But it didn't stop him from lighting a cigarette any time he needed one, despite the large warning sign on the oxygen tank that read: "No Smoking". *Oh, dad.*

And still, his body kept fighting long after the life he was defending had packed up and left because, let's face it, this was my stubborn, relentless, son-of-a-bitch, father (sorry Grandma).

He's drowning, I thought after hearing the news from Ethan. Drowning in his own fluids. Just like I feared. Slowly, painfully. This is how it ends?

"What are you telling me?" I asked Ethan, my heart punching my sternum like it wanted out.

"They can put him on life support... until you get here. But he begged me, and he made me promise. No machines. Whatever happens, don't let them hook him up."

The SUV kept humming north, but I went still. Highway white noise filled my skull.

"So..." he hesitated. And then the gut punch to end all gut punches. "I'm leaving it up to you."

Me?

The word ricocheted around the car. I stared at the headrest in front of me like it might

answer.

"Do you still want him alive when you get here?" Ethan asked, voice shaking. "Even if he can't... you know..."

I could feel the fear in his own chest through the phone. He didn't want to betray my dad's wishes. No machines, no tubes, no heroics, but he didn't want me to lose my goodbye either.

Later I learned that hours earlier my dad had repeated it clearly: no intubation, no wires, no last-ditch anything. When it's time, it's time. Of course the second he started coding, protocol sprinted in. My family had stepped out to breathe and reset. Doctors did what doctors are wired to do, save the body in front of them. They tried to suction and stabilize, to make space for air again. They failed.

When my family made it back, Lily said she'd never seen that face on our dad. His eyes were huge, pleading like a trapped animal while a tube slid past his teeth. The man who had stared down chemo and radiation and every bad hand cancer could deal... terrified. Finally, something scared him. He fought those nurses off the best he could, but all he could manage was begging with his eyes before they could sedate him.

And now the choice sat in my lap like a hot brick. Keep him tethered to machines until I got there or let him go on his own terms before I had the chance to say goodbye.

But I wasn't there yet because I was the one who left town. The one who wanted more than a barstool sermon and a tee time from that small town. The one who insisted on a different life. And somehow, I was the one holding the off switch? His end. His final minutes. After a lifetime of him holding the reins on mine?

I wasn't ready. Not for that call. Not for that job. Not for that kind of power.

How could I honor his boundary and still get the goodbye I had earned, if I'd earned it at all? Was it selfish to want that last look? Did I deserve it? I'd spent years fearing him, resenting him, petitioning the universe to turn him into a safer man. He chose substances and hobbies over us, again and again. Did I really get to be the daughter who had the right to keep him alive?

Seconds dragged like wet rope. Every version of him flickered behind my eyes; singing, dancing, that filthy laugh, the lectures, the holidays where we teamed up to roast my mom for being "too uptight." The dog wedding he officiated because I asked, and he loved an audience. The smoke. The beer. The absence that shaped me. Wanting him. Needing him. Hating him for making me want and need him. All of it surged at once, air thinning, chest tight, the highway a dull roar, my grandmother's tissue crinkling in the front seat, the dogs panting warm against my calf, and my father, hundreds of miles up the road, caught between breath and silence, waiting for me to choose.

"Kris?"

"Yeah?"

"We need to know, right now."

My heartbeat drowned the car, nothing but a piercing drumline in my ears. Words jammed in my throat, and then my mind slipped its seatbelt. I wasn't in the SUV anymore. I was a little kid in a sun-dappled forest, shoes slapping pine needles, skipping along. I glanced back and there he was, my dad, hands in his pockets, chin up, watching like a protective knight. Just us. And somehow, I felt safe. Like I could wander anywhere, carefree, and he'd be there like a warm shadow, catching anything the world threw.

I wanted that. God, I wanted that.

Fuck it.

"Keep him alive. I want to touch a warm hand, not a dead one."

"Okay."

Click. That was it.

Silence poured back in the car. I stared dead ahead, shaking, the road unspooling like tape. What had I just done? Did I buy myself one last chance at the dad I never had, like deathbed magic could turn him into my hero?

My grandma and Z murmured in the front seat like AM-radio static. I couldn't catch words, couldn't feel my legs. This wasn't supposed to be now. I thought I had more time. Lucy told me to come yesterday. Why didn't I? I'd waited for his mother, waited for the "right" moment like the universe hands out appointment slots for grief.

Is he suffering now because of me? Did I just prolong his pain? Is he still alive? Will I ever hear his voice again? Will I see his eyes? The way they softened when he couldn't find the words? Why is this happening to me? No one prepared me for this moment. This isn't fair. Why me?

So, yes, I kept my dad alive for me. To hold his hand one last time. To sit beside him without bracing for impact, for once in my life. Even if I never saw his eyes again, I needed his warmth. That presence. That goodbye. And I hated that I needed it. Hated how much I still needed my dad, one final time. But this time it was on my terms. No golf cart getaway, no beer, no mic. He had to stay put with me, and I had to stay put with him.

Outside, the sky bled gold into orange and purple, one of those California sunsets that tricks you into thinking pain takes a smoke break. My dad lived for sunsets. He'd call us out of the house to go see them like a two-alarm fire: "Girls! Look outside! Now!" As if we could scrapbook the sky if we all just paid attention.

I snapped a photo from the back seat of that sunset. My dad's final sunset. Proof. A timestamp that beauty still happened while everything else fell apart.

My dad was like the sun: warm, loud, impossible to ignore. Stare too long and it blinded you. Stand too close and it burned. Life-giving, but singed you in the same moment. Same man. Same math.

And during that drive the power sat with me. Life or death. Warmth or burn. He'd held that switch my whole life; suddenly, my thumb was on it. Maybe that's why I kept him a little longer, so I'd know how it felt, just for a moment, to hold the sun.

The next light wouldn't be golden; it would be fluorescent. The next sound, not wind through the window, but a monitor chirping on repeat. The next touch, not skin, but scratchy hospital blankets. The next smell: bleach, metal, and that singular smell of death.

I'm sorry, Dad. But fuck you. I need this.

CHAPTER 12
BIG DICK ENERGY

"It's not bragging if you can back it up."

—Muhammad Ali

The call I'd been waiting for at The Clinic finally came early that summer after my dad died.

"You're needed on set for one week to shoot five episodes."

Wait, what? I mean, hooray! But also… fuck.

I had a full dance card at The Clinic. Men timed their weeks around my schedule, not just for a machine and a protocol, but for the way I kept a room steady. I'd learned their tells: their bad jokes, the breath catch, the stare at the ceiling when shame crept in. I wasn't just a tech anymore; I was a pressure valve, a witness, the one woman in their orbit who didn't flinch at limp bodies or wobbly hearts. And a part of me loved being needed by these men.

But the call was the sign I'd begged the universe for. Proof the performer in me hadn't flatlined under nitrile gloves and progress notes. Could I keep both plates spinning right? Could I carry script sides in one hand, ultrasound gel in the other? I didn't know for sure, but I knew I had to try.

The very next day The Clinic hosted a training for doctors flown in from everywhere, lanyards swinging, coffee breath fogging the air. Same type of hotel-ballroom vibe where I'd first learned this stuff, loud HVAC, carpet that looked like static, projectors humming. Only now the chairs faced me.

Somehow, I was the draw: the girl with no initials after her name, the ex–car sleeper who used to measure self-worth by overdraft fees, now the VP of Dicks. Cedars-Sinai's head of urology had come to watch my hands work their magic. Mine. The ones that once shook audition sides now steadied a metal wand and a room full of nerves.

They expected technique; I gave them that. Mask here, gloves to the elbow, quadrant map, pressure, pace. But I built the session around the thing no one lists on a supply sheet: how to treat a dick like it's attached to a person. How to read a flinch. Name the shame so it loosens its grip. Shut up long enough for a man to say the true thing he'd been facing. Humanity, people!

"Do they teach this in med school?" I asked the room, half joke, half plea.

Blank stares. A few tilted heads. One dry chuckle.

They knew I was right. Maybe that was the point. Maybe they needed actors to teach doctors empathy. Show them how to hit their mark, listen harder than they speak, meet the scene partner where he was.

After demonstrating the technique I'd perfected on a couple of volunteer dicks (read: friends), I felt the old electricity rise in me, the same charge I get before a take. Okay, I thought. Maybe I really can do both. Maybe I do love both. Time would tell.

If my dad could see me now, he'd roll his eyes, throw out a scoff for show, and then, once no one was looking, beam. He loved a wild story as much as I did. I got my warped lenses from him. He'd secretly love that I was helping men with their dicks, and he'd clock the weight of it beyond the gag line. That was his thing: pretend it's a joke, feel it like a sermon. He might not brag to his buddies, but he'd laugh so hard he'd have to step outside...and that would be his version of proud, even if he couldn't say it to my face.

The day after the conference, I flew to Vegas. Cue $35 million Mandarin-language production with the logistics of a garage band. My Uber dumped me in a beige subdivision where every house looked copy-pasted and the baby trees were zip-tied to stakes, begging for groundwater. No welcome. No call sheet. Just 110 degrees panting on the pavement, a neighbor's dog throwing side-eye barks over a cinderblock wall, and me with a roller bag and a prayer.

The Airbnb door beeped me in and exhaled stale, Fabuloso air. The place felt staged for a crime reenactment: echoey tile, generic vertical blinds slicing light, a locked thermostat that thought suffering builds character. No people. No note. A lone water ring on the kitchen counter, a couch the color of defeat. I wandered room to room, heartbeat loud in the silence, until I spotted a few script pages face-down on a bed, Chinese characters like tiny marching ants, and a guitar leaning in the corner like an alibi. Okay. Either I'd found base camp, or I'd broken into the prettiest decoy in Clark County. The guitar talked me off the ledge: somewhere, a chill human with calluses on their fingers existed. Which meant work would, too.

On my first day, the transportation department was late to pick me up. Fine.

Then I opened my trailer to a convection oven with wheels—no AC, dead toilet, and a breadcrumb trail of script pages like someone fed my sides to a paper shredder. Still fine. But when no one called me to set until day three and the Assistant Director gave me mutha fuckin' ten minutes to create my character's look for the first time in hair, makeup, and wardrobe because they'd bungled call times again, my smile got tight. I'm a team player, not a miracle worker with a curling iron.

Normally this level of amateur hour would light my producer brain on fire. I had produced multiple projects, including a feature. Once you've been behind the camera, you can't unsee the errors some productions make when you're "just the actor." I knew how to run a set. Maybe not a $35M circus, but the basics aren't rocket science: keep people safe, keep people fed, keep people on schedule. We were zero for three. Stunts without padding, crafties with vibes only, and a schedule written in crayon.

But something in me had shifted since my dad died and since I became the VP of Dicks. I shelved my high standards and handed out grace like granola bars. I was just stupid-happy to be acting again. I decided to stay unflappable: nod, hit my mark, ignore the sweating makeup and the lukewarm water, do the scene. Even when I went home with purple constellations blooming on my shins from "light" stunts, I told myself: this is the dream, remember?

Call it my own Big Dick Energy; quiet, grounded, no power trip. Not the chest-thumping kind the higher-ups were flexing, but the kind you earn by surviving. I'd spent a year with every variety of dick in my latex-covered hands; I knew my value. On shaky days on set I gave myself a pep talk: these producers are lucky my very competent, very steady dick-fixing hands are moonlighting here. Then I laughed at myself, powdered my melting T-zone, and went to set.

The set was predictably patriarchal. Just a sausage party of producers, stunt guys, camera operators, and gaffers all trying to out-bro each other while the women hovered at hair, makeup, or on standby like well-behaved props. And there I was, parked in the middle of the bro-weather, carrying a delicious secret: weekdays, I held grown men's dicks while they cried and confessed the fears they wouldn't tell their priests. I had more field notes on the male ego than a shelf of graduate thesis and that secret sat in my pocket like a switchblade. I had power.

Between takes I'd listen to the peacocking; box-office stats, bench presses, car mods, over the hiss of fog machines and the tang of hot cables. Inside my head: *You're scared. Scared your dick isn't big enough, hard enough, frequented enough. Scared she's bored. Scared the best year of your life was three haircuts ago. That you peaked too soon. Scared you're irrelevant. And by the way, your resting heart rate and that sugar-free energy drink says, "ED with a side of denial."*

But I could also see the little boys under the tool belts: the nervous fingernail and cheek biting, the laugh that lingered a beat too long, the posture that begged, Am I doing it right? It softened me. With all my insider dirt, I'd forget I wasn't one of the guys; I was the woman holding the data set.

Sometimes I wanted to drop my job title just to watch the dominoes fall. I could script the reactions: shock, squint, joke, blanch, another joke to spackle the fear. Their pupils would do the math, scanning highlight reels and lowlight nights: Would she think I'm small? Babe, I've seen the whole museum of dicks—masterpieces, fridge art, and everything in between.

And honestly? It lit me up. Not to humiliate anyone, just to clock that I no longer flinched around men who used to own the room and my nervous system. I used to walk onto sets like this and shrink on contact: Am I young enough, thin enough, fuckable enough? Prey-brain. Now I padded in like a cat that knows where the exits are. Predator-brain. The laugh in my head? Full Ursula from *The Little Mermaid;* silky, villainous, delighted.

I wasn't casting them the way they cast me; I was triaging them like clients. The overtalkers, the protein-shake philosophers, the ring-tappers. I could spot who was compensating, who was glass-fragile, who probably needed a booster in the nightstand. They had no idea I could read them that fast. It felt like walking through an animal shelter and, without touching a single cage, knowing which sweetie nips. Then I'd smile and lay down a light flirt, just enough to scramble the signal. Not because I wanted something, but because I could. That's BDE: power without the shove, charm without the hunger. The quiet certainty you earn by walking through fire and coming out with your eyebrows intact. After hundreds of sessions, I felt like a dick shaman. Blessed be the dicks.

I flew home after shooting exactly one episode of what I lovingly called Dehydrated Dreams. Scheduling was a joke, so I brokered a truce with the producers: weekdays at The Clinic, weekends on set. Cue seven straight weeks of fifty-hour dick duty, Friday-night red-eyes, and two 12-hour Vegas shoot days back-to-back. No days off. My body ran on coconut water and adrenaline; my eyelids felt sandblasted; my brain sizzled like a tourist in July who "forgets" sunscreen. And still, I was buzzing. Tired, wrecked, happy. Alive.

Something shifted in me that summer and how I carried myself around men.

The longer I worked both at The Clinic and on set, the more I clocked the patterns. The puffed chests, the held breath, jokes as armor. Whether from the men on my treatment table, the men on my TV show set, the men out in the wild or even my male friends with presumably fully functioning dicks, a consistency in behavior revealed itself. Men in my orbit weren't fooling me anymore. I saw right through the facade and deep into the trapped boys who never got a manual. And by then I could sit with that knowing without flinching or judgment.

Then Trey walked into The Clinic. Late fifties, tall, gorgeous, African-American, dreads grazing broad shoulders. His voice landed low, like a bassline you feel in your ribs. He carried the kind of quiet that makes a room exhale. I pegged him for a yoga teacher, or some desert-retreat sage. He radiated I-have-seen-some-things-and-made-peace-with-them energy. If serenity wore cologne, it would have smelled like Trey.

That's a real man, I thought. *That's real Big Dick Energy. Trey knows who he is and isn't looking for anyone's approval or attention. What a thing of beauty to witness. Maybe he'd be willing to lead a class to teach these other guys? Does he have a son or younger brother?*

I wanted to be where Trey was, just existing in the moment. Calm, centered, certain of himself. Trey had nothing to prove and he felt so safe. He seemed safe within himself, and safe for me to be around as a result. He had that kind of energy that relaxed you the moment you entered his orbit. The kind that feels secure and warm like a cozy blanket.

Trey listened attentively as I explained the treatment to him. He told me he was at The Clinic because he'd lost his partner years before, but she came to him in a dream and told him it's time to find love again and rejoin the world. He had felt detached from sex in his grief and when he tried to pleasure himself, he couldn't stay hard. So he found us.

Trey was lovely and I wanted to help him immediately. But just as I pulled the sheet down to get to work, he shattered. Tears. Gasping. His body trembled like a plucked wire.

"Stop. Please," he choked.

I killed the machine, took his hand. "It's okay. Breathe with me." The paper on the table crackled under him; his breath snagged in short, panicked bursts. His pain felt deep. Guttural. I didn't have many experiences with panic attacks at that point, so I just instinctively tried to breathe with him until he could get back control. I nearly called the paramedics, but I didn't want to make things worse for him.

Eventually, his shoulders softened under my palm.

"I'm sorry," he whispered, drowning in apology.

He didn't need a device. He needed mercy. The man who'd glided in like still water now shook like a leaf. The mask was gone.

When he finally found words, they broke me. He still belonged to a ghost. He felt disloyal to a dead woman letting a stranger even look at his naked body. Touching felt like betrayal.

Oh, Trey.

I swallowed my emotions as best I could. As heartbroken as I felt for him, I didn't want to call attention to how he impacted me. Instead, I gently placed my hand on Trey's arm and told him there was no reason to force the treatment. He could pause his treatments until he was ready. And that if that day never came, I'd fight to get his money back. His dignity mattered more than any policy.

I felt protective of Trey's heart. Like he was now my child, and it was my responsibility to guide what was best for him. Once again, my savior complex was fighting for the spotlight.

He shook his head, "No, I'm here. I don't want to waste your time."

He nodded, then flinched at his own nod as if agreeing to care for himself embarrassed him. Shame flushed his face; he tugged the sheet higher, trying to hide a body that had just told the truth. He apologized again, then asked to continue. Pride wrestled grief in his eyes.

I gave him water. We waited. When he said "okay," we finished the treatment, gentle, slow, no heroics. The man who walked out looked smaller than the man who arrived. I hated that. I felt responsible, even though I wasn't. He never came back.

The experience with Trey sent me spiraling back to my dad. My father had his own brand of Big Dick Energy. It didn't fill a room; it filled a void. One carved by a childhood with divorces, religion used like a belt, addiction running the family like a union, suicide, and sexual abuse. So he built kingdoms where he could be king: at work, on the golf course, behind the karaoke mic. Places that saluted on command.

Home was chaos. Four daughters. Cats. Dogs. Hormones. Screaming.

He had little power there—when he actually was around. My mom kept the lights on, balanced the checkbook on her hip, and ran the family like air-traffic control: calm voice, twelve crises circling. I watched her crouch over a busted sprinkler, shim a wobbly table, user manuals spread on the dining table like a second set of hands. TV dads fixed things. In our house, Mom did. Not because she was single, but because she was abandoned, and we couldn't afford help. She resented it out loud and once told my dad flatly he'd become "irrelevant."

So when night fell, when the house got too loud or too tender and his illusion of control shook, he'd strike. Not with fists. With theater.

If he caught one of us hiccupping, it became a test.

"Let me hear you hiccup," he'd rumble, dropping his voice an octave like a spell, squaring up like a drill sergeant. Somehow, it always worked. Our hiccups vanished every time. As a kid, I thought he was magic. Later, I understood: fear clamps a chest faster than a paper bag.

The lectures were his Olympics. My God, the lectures. They didn't last an hour—they spanned seasons. My childhood was bookmarked by lectures the way normal kids remember holidays.

He'd find something, anything, to be disappointed in: I'd talked back; I'd left dishes wrong; I'd shown too much autonomy; I'd failed as an example to my sisters. Whatever the charge, I was summoned. Fuck. My whole body tensed at the doorway. Fight-or-flight lit up.

"Kristina. Get in here. Now."

I walked in on eggshells, sat small and still, prepared for the worst.

He planted himself in his chair, cigarette in one hand, beer in the other, puffing like a chimney and preaching like a prophet. Sometimes he knelt in front of me. Sometimes he leaned in from the ottoman, smoke curling between us. Always, he poked a finger into my chest, each jab meant to press the lesson deeper into my tiny soul.

I trembled, terrified of the man who was supposed to protect me.

My mom hovered in the doorway. "Bob, it's a school night."

He snapped and waved her off. "I'm not finished. And don't interrupt me again."

He hated being interrupted. When Mom ran interference, her voice shrank to a postage stamp. She loathed his dominion but didn't have the muscle in her throat to push back. She couldn't protect me, and I stopped trusting her to try.

He kept preaching. I wasn't a child anymore; I was his audience, his mirror for smudges. I was the good kid, maybe too good; the eldest who paved the road everyone else got to walk. I laid track while no one laid it for me.

At nine, GATE tapped me. The "Gifted and Talented Education" program you had to test into. Honor roll, trophies, ribbons: I stacked them like sandbags. The lectures still came. Not because I'd erred, but because he needed the floor. Maybe he wanted credit for my goodness, a fingerprint on my report card, proof he'd participated in my childhood.

I couldn't read the motive. Protect me from his mistakes, maybe, but I read the message: I was a failure-in-progress, a disappointment sprouting. Nothing could outrun the next sermon. He strung me on a balance beam over broken glass: keep perfect form or pay.

By the back half of his sermon, the booze outran his bravado. Beer twelve sanded down his consonants; his eyelids drooped to half-mast; his chin sagged until it kissed his chest. Mid-sentence, he drifted, a cigarette parked on the chair arm, the ember drawing lazy red circles like a bored firefly.

I knew the cue by heart. I waited for the snore: the deep, sawing-through-timber rumble that meant the coast was clear. Then I moved. Slow. Quiet. I'd learned the land mines after the one time I startled him, and he came up swinging. Never again.

I pried the cigarette from his fingers or rescued it where it teetered on the upholstery. Sometimes it had already tattooed a black crater; sometimes one more second and we'd be a tiki bar. I pinched the ember out, ran it under the tap, listened to that angry little hiss, and wiped the brown smear off my fingers with a dish towel that never came clean.

I was ten. Sometimes nine. Maybe eight. Too young to be the night-shift fire marshal, certified anyway. I didn't know how to strike a match; I knew how to smother one.

It became ritual: me making the house safe again, erasing heat he never noticed he'd left behind. Our pattern: I put out what he lit and pretended it was normal.

That's how he wielded power, not with rescues, but by crowding the air. He vacuumed the oxygen out of rooms until we breathed in sips. There was never quite enough space left for anyone else's pulse.

I learned my choreography for men from him: freeze first, appease second. Offer pieces of myself as peace offerings. Keep the weather inside men stable so the roof over me stayed put. I didn't learn to speak up; I learned to soundproof.

And then there's the maddening part. How do you square the man who kept me small with the man who trapped spiders in a glass and carried them outside like honored guests, who teared up at American Idol because a nineteen-year-old from nowhere finally got a shot? How do you forgive someone who never protected you for being someone who maybe, just maybe, never learned to protect himself?

That summer at The Clinic, men like Trey and Jack looked to me for answers. They came for comfort. For steadiness. And for the first time, I realized I had BDE. It wasn't borrowed or faked. It wasn't a role. It was mine, earned after years behind safety goggles I could finally take off.

I learned Big Dick Energy doesn't come from size, or from having a dick at all. It comes from owning your story. From surviving what should've broken you. From walking into rooms where people doubt you and making them believers.

Trey's BDE masked his biggest cracks. My dad's was fear-based – avoidant, combative, desperate.

My BDE came quietly. Through breath. Through stillness. Through knowing I could light a fire or walk away. I didn't need to scare the hiccups or erectile dysfunction out of anyone with a shaming lecture. I could let them be.

Maybe that's what my dad, in his twisted way, was trying to teach: power isn't always the loudest voice. Sometimes it's the one that listens, the one that can hold space for the pain of the same man who caused her pain. Sometimes the biggest dick isn't a dick at all. It's a woman finally unafraid to take up space and own her worth. When we redefine power as wholeness, the cycle breaks: men get to be human, women stop disappearing, and we choose connection over control and stop mistaking fear for love.

CHAPTER 13
DIGGING FOR DICKS

"It's not the size of the dick in the fight; it's the size of the fight in the dick."

—Inspired by Mark Twain

After a long summer split between filming the TV show and The Clinic, I finally wrapped filming in Vegas and settled back into my L.A. rhythm. The Clinic was officially booming. So booming, in fact, that it was time to train a new technician. A Dick Fixer Jr.

As possessive as I felt about being the one and only, my wrists, elbows, shoulders, and spine filed formal complaints. I grudgingly loosened my grip on the schedule to save my body (and a shred of sanity). It wasn't like nurses lined up for this specialty. We needed a very particular animal. We started hunting.

Meanwhile, money men started circling with franchise proposals and slick smiles. The possibility thrilled me. I'd helped build a real thing, not a temp job in spandex. I wore an honest-to-God title now: Vice President of Dicks.

And the money? Holy hell. I'd just cleared my first $10K take-home month. For a former starving artist who believed suffering proved I deserved an acting career, those paychecks scrambled my circuitry. I'd clung to the story that a full-time day job meant selling out, so I'd stayed broke on principle. Noble, but exhausting.

I'd tried the "normal job" route. In L.A., every interview started with, "You're not an actor, are you?" like they were asking about a felony. I once lied to land a personal-trainer gig at a fancy Santa Monica gym. Degree in exercise physiology, actual experience, and still, the only question that mattered was whether I'd ditch a client's weigh-in for a last-minute audition. I lasted a month. The lie curdled in my gut until I quit.

Then I waited tables. Not that I had experience, just the mythology that actors must be servers. It wrecked me. Not the labor, the contempt.

I had a college degree, and the shitty tips made me feel like pocket lint. One windy morning, a gust rattled the front door while I Windexed a window and—SNAP—my back went out. I finished the shift hunched over and sweating from the pain. I couldn't walk for six months. Oh, how humbled, depressed and miserable to be immobile from a damn gust of wind. If the universe had a Post-it for me, it read: Not this.

I hustled instead. I opened a training business, rode it through the 2008 recession, then patchworked gigs: house-sitting, dog-sitting, nannying, bookkeeping, events, modeling, coaching kids. I avoided going "all in" anywhere so everyone knew what I really did, even when "really" meant sleeping in my car twice because at least the debt collector didn't live there.

Then came The Clinic and the dicks that came with it. What started as a part-time gig (read: favor) turned into a life. Fulfillment terrified me and set me free. I could pay bills early. Buy my own clothes. Take my dog to the vet without bargaining with God. Seeing a big number in my bank account changed how I moved through the world.

But money also triggered my control issues. If someone else paid, I felt owned. I'd rather live out of my trunk than owe a man rent. I'd tried letting one bankroll me once; when he weaponized it, I swore never again. So I overworked, overgave, overspent. Independence had a choke chain, and even with Z I clung to the bill. Being financially in charge felt safer than being cared for.

That grip on control didn't stop at my bank account; it lived in my body, too. Balance felt impossible. I chased bigger paydays, like they were fleeting, but the hours at The Clinic chewed me up. I stood in heels: my uniform, my armor, because sensible shoes didn't fit the character I'd crafted. After hours, I punished myself with CrossFit which made me lean but not strong, fast and frail. I wanted real power, the kind that made predation bounce off. Once you've been assaulted, you scan rooms for exits forever.

So I tried triage. A $35 Thai massage near my house when I could crawl there. My right side, from wrist to neck, screamed daily. The device kicked like a weld gun. I knew the diagnosis before I admitted it: RSI. Repetitive Stress Injury. We saw them all the time at the physical therapy clinic I worked at in college. Repetitive motion, zero recovery. Pride told me to push through the tennis elbow. The Clinic, our clients, these results; they were mine. Even if the bill came due in my joints.

Meanwhile, life refused to wait its turn. My mom moved into Lucy's back house with a tenth of her things and only one dog; the rest went to storage with my dad's ghost. I clocked it, nodded, compartmentalized and went back to the calendar of dicks. No time to help my mom grieve and my compassion ran out of stamina.

And right on cue, Vlad waddled into The Clinic.

He wore a gold chain, a thick Russian accent, and a permanent scowl. Cash man.

Once, I watched an interview with James Gandolfini on I*nside the Actor's Studio with James Lipton.* Lipton asked him how he maintained the high level of frustration that Tony Soprano was so famous for throughout the filming. James responded with, "I put a rock in my shoe every day." Genius.

A shoe with a rock in it felt like Vlad to me. Just a low level of irritability happening all the time. Vlad and my dad, sober. Always ready to snap.

I had to handle his consultation alone because my bosses were out of town.

"You the boss?" Vlad smirked. "No one else?" He was clearly uncomfortable with the idea of me being in charge.

"Nope," I said, with a tight smile. "Just me."

He laughed through his nose. "You too pretty for this job."

I'm sorry, do you need me to get ugly real quick so you can take me seriously?

I'd spent my whole life trying to prove I had more to offer than my looks. That I had a brain, a skillset, a soul. And here we were again. Yet another man trying to make me small because he didn't know how to make himself feel big.

Don't ruin my newfound hope in men, Vlad. Not today.

Vlad questioned everything: the treatment, the science, the price, and of course, me. He asked if there was a money-back guarantee (there wasn't). He exhausted me with his lack of confidence. We had the Yelp reviews. We had the professional facility. We had been successful for months. What else did he need? Vlad had been convinced enough over the phone with my boss to make it into The Clinic, yet something about me wasn't enough for him to be sold without a fight.

Stay soft, Kristina. Stay professional. Don't let him bulldoze your confidence. You know who you are. He has no power over you.

I wondered if the universe was sending me some final boss test to see just how far I'd go. Would I resort to my previous unhealed self and shrink to his challenging and domineering presence? Would I overcompensate to make him feel small as a way to gain control? I was battling his ego and all of my daddy issues at once.

Eventually, after a full 45 minutes of Russian suspicion and passive-aggressive interrogation, Vlad threw down $6,000 in cash and said, "Okay. Let's do it."

Exhale. I won. I bested my own ego and his. Whew.

I walked him into the treatment room and gave him the rundown. I'd be back in a few minutes while he undressed. He shook his head, still in disbelief about what was about to go down.

I left him there, despite himself.

If I'm honest, I still didn't want to see his dick. His energy repelled me; he instantly joined the very short list of clients I dreaded. But I knew his type. He was my dad's cousin in spirit with the same user manual. That puffed-up certainty that says, "I've never done this, but I definitely know more than you. You're a woman. I'm a man. It's science."

That rehearsed authority covering a paper-thin center was too familiar. My dad flexed with lectures, little stabs, and strategic disappearances. Vlad flexed with cash and suspicion. Different props, same engine: fear dressed as swagger.

I walked back in, snapped my gloves with a bit too much confidence. His belly shook with a deep patronizing laugh.

Oh, no you don't, Vlad.

This was my room. My mutha fuckin' arena. If Vlad wanted to fight dirty, I'd play by his rules just to tame him.

Strap in, you arrogant clown, this is gonna hurt. You're about to be my bitch.

I prepped my space and my soul for the next forty-five mins with this dude without a word. I knew the next moment usually confirmed or contradicted my hunch about a man—the reveal of the source material for all that personality. Let's see this cocky prick's dick.

I lifted the edge of the drape… Paused… Looked again… Nothing.

Um…

No theatrics, no exaggeration, there was simply… no dick in sight.

Vlad's dick had retracted up into his body like a frightened turtle on its first day at the zoo. He was so overweight, and his penis so small, that it had disappeared entirely. Poof. Gone.

Ah, come on Vlad! Don't be that stereotypical dude who has a huge ego and a small dick. The lifted truck revving his engine to try to get attention that he knows his dick never could. I'm trying to champion men right now. Don't make me retract my findings and evolve backward. Don't be a dick without a dick, Vlad!

The situation was a first for me. I'd treated big men with small equipment before, proof that body size doesn't predict dick size. But at least with my previous clients, there had been something, anything, to work with. Their dinky dicks were at least outside of their body. With Vlad, he was my show-me-where-the-problem-is-because-I-can't-find-it dick. I was on a full-blown dick scavenger hunt. The Where's Waldo of Wiener Town.

So, I did what any emotionally resilient, physically broken, Vice President of Dicks would do: I went digging.

I went full-glove spelunking. I had to use my entire forearm just to lift and maneuver Vlad's massive testicles, ones that felt like microwaved yams, out of the way. They blended ever so gracefully into his thigh folds, which made navigating around them nearly impossible. I sweated until I was drenched. So did he. The room smelled like anxiety and cheap cologne.

Vlad was the reason I hunted down longer gloves. After treating him, I wanted gloves that covered my forearms, so no part, and I mean zero part of my skin would ever come into contact with any part of my clients' dick, balls, or pubes, ever again.

But I didn't have those damn gloves in that moment. It was our first appointment. So, my delicate forearm skin made contact with this miserable Russian, humid Humpty Dumpty nut sack. I swallowed my tiny scream.

Fuck! Why me? Was this some cosmic penance for every time my dad made me feel like I'd earned punishment? Anyone, please, beam me out of this nut-sack labyrinth.

And then... Vlad giggled. A quick, high, startled chirp—pure helium. When I looked up, a little boy stared back: eyes shiny, cheeks tight, the silent plea of someone caught with a hand in the cookie jar. Don't tell. Not this. Not me.

Words failed him, the way they'd always failed my dad. The treatment had cracked something he'd spent a lifetime soldering shut. I wanted to hate him; I couldn't. The bravado fell off like a costume, and all I saw was a man hauling around a secret that lived where his body should have been simple. His missing dick made me soften. I pitied the way he moved through the world with a vanishing act between his legs.

I couldn't stop wondering how a man lives with an innie dick. How did he pee? Hands pressed in like he's coaxing out a shy turtle? How did he masturbate—with tongs? How did he have sex, or even keep things clean? My brain ran the logistics, then, because I'm deranged and curious, I staged the whole choreography in my head. *Was he here for me to fix his dick... or to locate it first?*

A real deal micropenis. *Is he looking to me to find it, tend it, coax it into daylight? Like a lone miner stuck in a cave, sending smoke signals from the depths of the earth. Not a rescue, but more of a search party with a headlamp and a clipboard. This is definitely a first.*

As I dug into Vlad physically and metaphorically, the pattern clicked. Vlad was every man who'd hit on me before I could read the tells: the widened stance, the square jaw, the "listen, sweetheart" cadence, the charm with a threat baked in. And here he was, flattened under a paper drape, absolutely powerless. I stayed gentle. A year ago I would've recoiled. Now I stayed open. That was new for me.

And his posture wasn't only personal; it was cultural. He came from an era and world where masculinity wasn't suggested, it was enforced. Dominance as dialect. You don't ask for respect; you perform it at full volume.

Mid-stroke, a line I love, floated up: Powerful people don't need to tell you they're powerful. Exactly. All that bluster? Just noise to drown out the hum of panic. There was no universe where a man with a disappearing penis didn't carry a daily ache of shame for the body he'd been issued. No shade to God, but the allocation felt cruel.

After that first, deeply uncomfortable appointment, I didn't know if Vlad would come back. Yet week after week, he showed up. And each week, a little more of him surfaced, both the man and the anatomy. He was a little more Vlad, and a little more dick. He scoffed less. He cursed less. A real smile started to creep in and stay. His guard never dropped all the way, but it didn't have to. I could see what lived beneath it. I was proud of him.

I was proud of me, too. I didn't let his attitude calcify me. I didn't retreat or shrink. Like exactly what Vlad's dick needed, I stood tall, heels and all. I held my boundary. I held my compassion. I did for Vlad what I could never do with my father. I stayed soft in the presence of hardness. I kept my power without going cold.

Vlad reminded me not every arrogant man is a monster. Some are boys who never learned how to say, "I'm scared," "I don't know," or "I need help."

I'd finally seen past the costume men like Vlad, and my father, were trained to wear. And now? I wasn't afraid to look men in the eye, even the peacocks. The smallest dicks deserve help, too. And even with my back screaming and my forearms lit up, somehow, I'd become their champion.

CHAPTER 14
DICK DAMAGE

"Even the strongest erections can be brought down by a well-placed scar."

—allegedly Nietzsche, but definitely not

The most broken dick I ever faced was Marco's. Not metaphorically broken: physically. He became my greatest project and, somehow, my biggest win.

Unlike Vlad's disappearing act, Marco's problem sat right there on the table entirely exposed.

Early fifties, handsome, vaguely famous, Marco arrived at The Clinic like any other client with a polite smile, quick paperwork, no hints from my bosses that I was about to meet the medical equivalent of a boss level. He didn't warn me either.

By then I'd developed my own little dick diagnostic: a quick squeeze at the start of our first session to test the health of their tissue. My thumb and forefinger gently around the shaft, light pressure, like checking a nectarine for give. I'd start at the base and work my way up until just below the head. Clinical, not creepy. I was testing for bounce. Healthy tissue answers you; it yields and springs back. When it doesn't, when it stays stubborn and still, that's scar tissue. Fibrosis. Sometimes calcification. The body's overzealous repair crew pouring concrete over a pothole.

With Marco, the entire end of this shaft felt like gravel. Like a cluster of tiny pebbles buried under his skin. No flex. No movement. It felt... dead.

What he had was textbook Peyronie's disease, though Marco had never heard the term. Most guys hadn't. They just thought it was deformed.

Peyronie's happens when microtears in the tunica albuginea, the sheath around the erectile chambers, heal wrong. One bad bend, or a lifetime of small insults, and the collagen goes rogue. Scar tissue forms, then hardens. The scar tissue shrinks and pulls, curving the erection, shortening it, sometimes hurting like hell; sometimes it just kills sensation and blood flow. In the worst cases, the scar calcifies. Stone where flesh should be.

Marco insisted he was "fine." He could get "sort of hard." But survival wasn't the bar. Not on my table. Not if I was involved. Function without feeling is just a pulse; these guys came for connection.

I stared at Marco's armored glans and thought, *How in God's name did we get here?* Was he into smash-bang kink? Did he shut a car door on it? A blowjob with a plot twist? The forensic questions in my head were not helpful, but they were loud.

I did know one common culprit: injectables. When pills stop working, some urologists prescribe shots like alprostadil or tri-mix. Moments before sex, the man stabs his own penis to dilate vessels and pull blood in. Romantic, right? Over time, pierce the same spot and the site calcifies. Repeat, and a plaque forms; repeat, and the angle arrives. Cue the bend, the numbness, the shame spiral.

So yeah, by the time these guys landed on my table, most were desperate for an alternative to regular self-harm for pleasure.

I had no formal Peyronie's training, and absolutely no guarantee I could help someone this far into their dick damage. With general calcification scattered here and there, I usually won us back sensation and flow by following the standard protocol. Marco's case made my stomach drop. Would I hurt him? Waste his money? Fail him? The honest answer: I didn't know. The truer answer: I wasn't built to walk away.

Which is how I treated every man in my life. Fixer on arrival. I'd been loving men like they were group projects since high school, morphing, shrinking, overperforming, abandoning pieces of myself to prove I was worthy enough to keep. I called it loyalty. A therapist would call it anxious attachment. Tomato, tomahto, daddy issues either way.

It wasn't just Marco I wanted to save. It was every ghost I'd ever chased.

My "type" wasn't height or hair; it was heat signature. Charming, slippery, and attentive until they weren't. My dating pool cracked open just enough to make me swear there was more to them, then closed the curtain. Their inconsistency became my challenge. Their coldness, my dare. If I could be the one who made a man stay, I could rewrite the past. But I wasn't chasing men; I was chasing my dad.

My dad was the original unavailable man. Brilliant, hilarious, magnetic, then distant, cruel, patronizing. As the oldest daughter, I absorbed it all. If I wanted love, I had to earn it: be capable, be helpful, be good. There was no room for my fear or sadness, so I carried them like contraband. "Strong" became code for unprotected.

Oldest daughters learn to anticipate needs, not voice them. We manage chaos; we don't receive care. So when love arrived in a costume of inconsistency, I recognized it. I could show up for uncertainty; I could not locate safety. I'd never had it.

My first long-term boyfriend after high school was a near-copy of my father. Let's call him Luke. Luke looked perfect on paper: smart, athletic, the quiet alpha everyone deferred to. Behind a closed door, he turned volatile. He got in my face and screamed. He called me a whore if a waiter made eye contact with me. I built him a backstory to excuse it: a mother who left, a cruel stepmom, a dad who worked himself into absence. Pain made him sharp; I told myself compassion made me stay.

My first semester of college, every Friday, I white-knuckled 400 miles home up the I-5; two gas stations, one Big Gulp, highway buzzing under bald tires, because keeping him calm had become my job. I didn't make friends at school. I didn't build a life. I managed Luke. I kept a running list of ways to be smaller, sweeter, untempting. Nothing in him changed, no matter how much I did.

Two years in, I couldn't take it anymore. A couple weeks after I finally broke up with him, he drove a group of friends home from a party, completely sober, and made a reckless choice that cost two of our friends their lives. Two kids, 19 and 20 years old.

I blamed myself. From 400 miles away, I still let the guilt collar me. If I hadn't left, maybe... He agreed. He told me their blood was on my hands. A sick part of me nodded.

While Luke waited to hear if manslaughter charges would stick, I performed penance. I let him smash my keepsakes. I watched him burn my high school photo albums in a trash can on the patio, the plastic edges warping, faces bubbling, my past crackling to ash. When he slammed my head against the wall, I told myself it was an accident. When he grabbed my arms, I said I'd startled him. He threatened to kill himself and I went on high alert, sleeping with one eye open and my shoes by the door.

One night he ran three miles to the ocean and dove in, roaring that he wanted to die because of me. I chased him down the wet sand in jeans and a sweatshirt, lungs burning, salt air needling my throat. I waded in up to my ribs, teeth chattering, begging him to come out while strangers pretended not to stare. I was twenty, soaking, terrified and somehow convinced I deserved this.

After months of court hearings, and the worst abuse I had seen from Luke, he was convicted of manslaughter and sentenced to six months in county. I moved home for the summer so I could orbit the jail. I wrote him a letter every day so there'd be mail with his name on it each morning. Every Wednesday, on visiting days, I sat under flickering fluorescents on a metal stool that rocked, pressed a greasy handset to my ear, and watched his eyes through smeared plexiglass harden into interrogation. "Who are you fucking on the outside?" I learned the stamp ink takes two days to fade off your skin. I learned the vending machines only take exact change. I learned how to steady my voice while my stomach flipped. I learned not to dress too provocatively, but still look like I tried for him, just the way he wanted it.

The day he was released was the day I left for the study-abroad program in Spain. I picked him up from jail at 3 a.m., his plastic belongings bag rustling in my passenger seat, dropped him off and drove to the airport at 5 a.m. I made it to Granada, but I never arrived. His calls detonated every night across the Atlantic. Rage, apology and rage again. I lasted for nearly six months before I signed the withdrawal form with a shaking hand, packed the suitcase, and flew home to try to make it better between us.

I returned to him. My "reward" was more of the same: manipulation, control, the kind of infidelity I absorbed like a fine for leaving. I told myself loyalty required endurance. I told myself that if I could hold on long enough, he'd soften. Instead I shrank. Classes slipped. Scholarships wobbled. My part-time job asked if I was okay; I lied, because I was the girl who took care of people, not the girl who needed help.

Five years bled out like this, a thousand paper cuts, a handful of bruises, and the low-grade terror that he might show up and finish what he threatened. Even after I finally left for good, I flinched at unfamiliar footsteps in hallways. A small, twisted corner of me still believed I had it coming.

Luke was my father in a younger body. Volatile love, conditional safety, attention weaponized as control. I didn't date a man; I reenacted a childhood. And I stayed because I thought surviving it meant I was "good."

After Luke came the good man. Maybe too good. Cameron. Cameron was the man I should've married. Kind, steady, hot and hilarious. Like too much in one package. He adored me out loud. He had an incredible family and upbringing. Stable and solid in every sense of the word.

Cameron lived for the moment. He booked romantic dinners on the San Francisco Bay for no reason; heat lamps clicked on, string lights blinked awake, fog licked the windows while he watched my face like a favorite movie. On Saturdays we crashed strangers' quinceañeras just because the DJ was killing it. We spun under paper flowers until my calves burned, and the aunties clapped us toward the dessert table like we belonged there.

We also had sex in a stand-up tanning booth in San Diego because we knew the owner and... well, we were twenty-something geniuses. The plastic door rattled, the bulbs hummed, coconut-scented heat wrapped around us, and ten minutes later he emerged with second-degree grill marks on both cheeks. Our weekend ended with him face-down in the back seat, an ice pack tucked between his butt like a sad sandwich, while I laughed for six hours up the I-5 praying every pothole wouldn't make him yelp. Ridiculous? Yes. Worth it? One thousand percent. That story still lives rent free in my brain.

With Cameron, I felt worshipped: alive, sparkly, safe. And that's when my wiring shorted. His steadiness made me suspicious. Predictability felt like a trick door. He couldn't understand why I kept trying to fix a family with a father who treated me like collateral damage. He wanted marriage and kids and a future with calendar invites. I took one look at the idea and my chest locked. Safety made me itch. Consistency read as boredom. I scanned the floor for trapdoors because that's what love had taught me to do.

Cameron offered a soft place to land; I didn't know how to land. I didn't feel worthy of something permanent or gentle. After four beautiful, confusing years, I left. It hurt, the clean kind of hurt you feel when you know you're walking away from kindness, not chaos, but I was too unsettled to stay. I told myself I needed to grow, to evolve, to find the part of me that could actually receive what he kept handing me for free. I didn't feel worthy. Not yet.

Cameron should've been the one that got away. Instead, I was the one who walked. Not because he lacked anything, but because I did: the ability to trust easy love.

Instead of soul searching and healing my relationship with my dad or any of the abuse I endured or why I rejected the perfect man who wanted to hand me everything, months later, I quickly fell into another relationship with a man who filled the gaps that Cameron couldn't. I found an emotionally intelligent artist. We'll call him Adam.

Adam arrived like relief in a cardigan: introverted, quick-witted, brilliant. He wasn't conventionally gorgeous, which tricked me into thinking I held the power. He spoke "feelings" fluently, admired my art out loud, and made space for the version of me I'd been hiding. We made things together: short films, plays, plans. I felt seen, understood, curated for the first time.

But his care had fine print.

Adam's help always came pre-assembled with hex keys and hidden screws. He solved problems before I finished describing them, slid his credit card across the table, and tucked the receipt into his pocket like a deed. He presented himself as emotionally available, intellectually superior, and, most importantly, financially in control. Every yes had a thread attached. Tug it, and the whole room moved his way.

What looked like generosity functioned like collateral. What looked like partnership operated like a quiet takeover. I didn't notice the handoff at first; I just woke up one day and realized the keys to my life lived on his ring. My money? Gone. My calendar? Negotiable. My voice? Whispered. I wasn't a girlfriend; I was an acquisition with great potential.

His manipulation didn't roar; it murmured. He played soft, apologetic, shy. Then he'd tilt the chessboard: a sulk here, a sigh there, a perfectly timed "I was only trying to help," and suddenly I was the ungrateful one. He offered solutions the way a spider offers a place to rest.

I stayed because he framed leaving as reckless and staying as love. Because I had no savings, no net, and a self-worth measured in IOUs. Because some part of me still believed I needed a custodian, not a partner.

When control slipped, he escalated and whispered threats of suicide shaped like ultimatums. The room shrank. My breath did too. That was the moment the part of me that still wanted to live finally got loud. I ran. Couches, then my car. Freedom tasted like stale coffee and borrowed blankets, but it was mine.

Adam wasn't a hurricane like Luke; he was a fog bank, easy to drive into, impossible to navigate, and somehow you still ended up crashing on his terms. I left that relationship without money, without a plan, but with the clearest truth I'd had in years: help that costs your selfhood is not help.

Between the long-term relationships, I had flings and crushes, sure, but I was wired as a serial monogamist. Dating felt like homework with no answer key: care just enough to learn a man's habits and maybe his dick, but not enough to bother with his middle name.

Plus, when I tried dating, I tended to want the men who didn't want me; the unavailable, the projects, the emotionally stunted, the self-destructive, the charmingly avoidant. If a man liked me right away, I didn't trust it; something had to be broken so I could fix it. The chase felt like love because that's what my dad taught me: a life of almosts and auditioning.

Worse than not trusting a man's interest, I still didn't know how to say no. Not clearly, safely, or without fear. I said yes to make men go away. I gave time, attention, and too often my body not from desire, but survival. Sober since high school me still nodded yes when every cell wanted to leave. At nineteen, I woke up under a freeway overpass in Vegas at four a.m. after being date-raped. Discarded. Terrified. Ashamed, like it was my fault.

I'd learned that saying 'no' could get you hurt and telling anyone what was happening might make it worse. No one was coming to protect me. Not even my dad, especially not my dad. I sanded down my discomfort to cushion theirs. Gold star in people-pleasing; failing grade in self-protection.

All through my twenties, I outsourced my worth. Men's moods were my performance reviews. Attention read as love, anger passed for investment, and suffering felt like a group project with my name on it. Spoiler: no rescue team was en route, least of all me.

Call it "daddy issues" if you want, but the longer name is an attachment wound. My first template for love was inconsistent and loud, so my nervous system got licensed to fly in turbulence: love must be earned, safety means managing someone else's weather, and attraction needs a little danger to feel real. That wiring doesn't make you broken; it makes you trained. Until you retrain it, you keep choosing the familiar over the healthy and calling it chemistry. Cute theory; brutal results.

Then thirty rolled in and Saturn showed up with a clipboard, a citation book, and a "we need to talk." Time to rewire. For those who follow the stars, Saturn Return, better known as, the cosmic HOA letter returns to its same place in orbit as when you were born to kick your ass. Astrologers say Saturn governs structure, responsibility, and hard lessons. In plain English? It's a cosmic wake-up call. It's when you're forced to reconfigure who you are, what you stand for, and how you want to live. For me, that meant facing the truth: I didn't want to just survive anymore. I wanted to live. I didn't want to be a pinball in a vintage pinball machine, knocking into things without direction and trying to stay in the game as long as possible. I wanted more meaning from my career, my day jobs, my family and my partnership. I just didn't know how to get there.

Then Z came along. Safe, sweet, simple Z. We started as friends, but with his persistence and charming innocence, we became a real thing. Z became a place I could settle into where my nervous system could calm, and I could receive love from a man without strings or control. But unlike with Cameron, I could actually receive the consistent love Z freely gave. And it was beautiful. Until it wasn't.

Even the safe men like Z or Cameron become unsafe when you are bringing your own unhealed shit to the partnership. Shit I had no idea I was still carrying. So I made Z the projection of all my unhealed wounds. Determined to fix in him what was broken in me.

And maybe in The Clinic with Marco's broken dick, the one I pressed and prodded and bled, was a turning point for me, now, in my mid-thirties. Maybe this was one time where my obsession with saving others could actually give me back a piece of myself.

Marco's dick became my greatest project. We worked our asses off to make him hard. He showed up, session after session, even when I made him bleed. I pinned the gold tip to those rock-bed plaques, and his skin would split; he'd jerk and yelp, and I'd steady him, one hand on the machine, the other on his shoulder, talking him through it like a flight attendant in turbulence. Numbing cream? Cute. It was lip balm on a brushfire. To break that scar, I had to turn the dial up, and he had to meet me there. If he wanted feeling back, he was going to have to walk through while I held his hand.

It took time, but the needle finally found a groove. Blood answered. Sensation flickered. His dick didn't turn into a movie montage; it just started working again. Not perfect, but functioning. And that felt like a win for both of us. A place we could settle. Not settle for but settle with.

Somewhere in there, the metaphor tapped me on the shoulder. I didn't need a flawless man or an unscarred one. I needed someone good enough to keep choosing me, without begging, bargaining, or running a loyalty program for my pain. Not love I had to audition for. Not sex I had to earn. Reciprocity or bust. And for that to happen, I had to become the steady one first; the woman who could model the love she wanted and tolerate the quiet that comes with safety.

In the end, the most broken dick I ever had wasn't Marco's, or my exes', or even my dad's. It was mine, the metaphorical portal into my own mess. My dick wound. The hairline fractures in my worth, the scar tissue around my "no," the numbness I'd called strength. No gold tip could touch that. It needed a different kind of medicine: therapy, honesty, silence, prayer, time. A full-body reboot. A spiritual awakening dressed up as a sex lesson.

CHAPTER 15
DREAMS VS. DICKS

"The best adventures are like the best dicks… dangerous enough to make you question your safety."

—Me, again

A couple of weeks into fall, the director from the Chinese TV series called, breathless. "They fired the entire American production company and moved the show to Saipan."

The fuck is that?

"It's an island!" he squeaked, delighted with his own news. "The producers loved your performance so much, they've extended your part. We need you next week. You have to come. It will be amazing!"

He cheered like a fan after a buzzer-beater, and I stood there like the ref waiting on a replay. Did I even have enough scenes for anyone to "love my performance"? I'd rolled around in Vegas desert dust like a champion and stayed charming between takes, sure, but my role was tiny, and the plot was… unclear.

Still, more episodes meant more money and more time doing the thing I really loved—acting. It was "only a week." I'd left The Clinic for a week before and made it work. What was the worst that could happen?

Even if they were inventing reasons to fly me out, my younger self would've fainted at the headline: Tropical Island. TV series. They want more of you. That same girl who hid in her mom's classroom for a year because she was bullied and had no friends, who could barely believe she was worthy of anything—now a six-figure-earning dick fixer with an actual invitation to paradise.

But The Clinic tugged on the other sleeve. My clients. My calendar. My dicks. Dreams on one line, erections on the other.

So I did what any woman with trauma history does when an unknown island whistles from the dark: I Googled. "Where the hell is Saipan?"

There it was, a tiny pinprick in the middle of the Pacific Ocean. The map icon was bigger than the land. I had to zoom all the way in to find it.

Saipan, part of the Northern Mariana Islands, a U.S. territory north of Guam.

Tinian, another tiny island nearby, turned out to be where the atomic bombs had been staged during WWII. Not exactly a bedtime story, but history rarely is.

I couldn't believe I never heard of this place. And I loved maps. Loved knowing where I was in relation to everything else, so I could feel in control and breathe. I'd been driving my mom around since I was fifteen; her panic attacks and bridges didn't mix, so I had to know where I was going. I became the family's freeway whisperer. Even teammates' parents tossed me keys and kids for tournament weekends since we had the minivan and could haul so many kids at once. I learned to float a minivan through storms like a tugboat from a young age.

If I agreed to go to Saipan it would be the farthest I'd gone from home since that college year in Spain. Thankfully, I had just renewed my passport for a Clinic trip to Cabo San Lucas, Mexico. The bosses wanted to celebrate the successful summer at The Clinic by treating us and our significant others to a wild weekend getaway. I think they just wanted to go to Cabo on the company's dime. Fine, I'd shake my ass for good music anywhere, but Spring Break energy as a sober person wasn't my thing. Z and I played along as best we could with our dwindling connection. Even the humidity and lack of responsibility couldn't make our sex life reignite.

After hours of researching the island and the cost of abandoning my clients yet again, I accepted the offer to live my dreams in paradise. My bosses reluctantly agreed to give me the time off from The Clinic. I had just started training someone new to take over the operations duties I tried to squeeze in between clients. Still, I remained the only technician. Not because we weren't looking for another, but because it wasn't easy to find someone else who wanted to do my job. The couple of nurses we hired and I trained each found themselves struggling to feel comfortable in the job. Fair. It wasn't for everyone, even if they actually had medical training. Plus, I wasn't ready to hand over my clients to someone who was "just okay". I felt protective of these men and what I had built. The Clinic ran on ritual and care; I'd built both. But the dream called, and I answered.

The plane ticket hit my inbox the day before I left. Chaos chic. Very Vegas of the producers. I didn't know who booked it or where they found my info, but it was real. I had a real ticket to head west, halfway across the world.

I packed twenty minutes before the Uber arrived, one carry-on. I didn't want my epileptic dog, Gus, to see the suitcase and tip into a seizure. He'd learned to associate luggage with me disappearing from that summer of traveling every weekend. Z had carried the fallout more than once, long weekends, long nights.

I flew to Honolulu, Hawaii first. I hadn't been back to Hawaii since the family's one true vacation to Oahu in 2010, the year after my mom's early retirement. They wanted Waikiki neon lights and Mai Tais; I wanted a remote green coastline and quiet. My country mice family wanted bustle; me, the city mouse, wanted space.

That trip included the standard Denton family mayhem of drunken sibling blowups on the beach and parental bickering. We stumbled onto a karaoke patio. My dad begged me to sing. I did "Black Velvet"; he crooned Sinatra. The crowd ate out of our hands. It was the biggest stage we'd ever shared, an outdoor lounge stuffed with sunburnt tourists.

"You did that!" he slurred, proud. "That's my big girl!"

He high-fived like he'd discovered me, women sidling up to gush, and he basked as if paternal excellence could be proven in applause. He wore my talent like a medal. You're welcome, Dad.

From Honolulu I boarded an eight-and-a-half-hour flight to Guam. Below us: water, then more water, then a horizon made entirely of water. It rattled me. I'd already flown twenty-seven times that year, between L.A., Vegas, and Cabo, but the open ocean still set off alarms. Over-the-ocean flights always did. I tried to focus on an old man behind me stomping his feet the whole flight; I cursed him until I realized he was preventing blood clots. I stomp when I travel now. I think of him and apologize in advance to everyone within earshot.

I crashed at a questionable-looking hotel in Guam that smelled like mildew and bleach had made a resentful baby. Karaoke thumped below my room all night. Normally, I'd be tempted to eavesdrop. After nearly twenty-four hours awake, I just wanted silence.

By morning I boarded the only flight to Saipan, a toy plane with twenty-something seats and windows that made the world look hyperreal. The water below was impossible: glassy, neon, a screensaver come to life. I took too many photos like the wide-eyed American tourist I was.

At Saipan's small airport, an adorable Bangladeshi cab driver held a marker-scrawled sign with my name. First time I'd ever had a sign. He grinned. I took a photo. He gave me a thumbs-up. For a second, it felt like I hadn't made a mistake. It felt official. Like the most A-list treatment I could get in the middle of nowhere.

The driver rattled his little diesel cab forty minutes north to my "hotel." The building looked like it had been assembled by ambitious high schoolers. The air smelled once again like bleach wrestling mold and losing. My room had no A/C, no fridge, and questionable Wi-Fi. The heat pinned me to the mattress and melted all my make-up. The isolation scrambled me as I awaited my next direction from... anyone. Technically U.S. soil, but Saipan didn't feel like it. I needed an anchor—someone, something familiar to tell me I hadn't floated off the map.

Production ran two units and funneled everyone to one Chinese buffet for every meal: breakfast, lunch, dinner, copy/paste menu. I arrived starving and found nothing I could eat. Vegan, gluten-free, sugar-free, seed-oil-free in Saipan translated to "eat rice or cry." It was not a moment for bougie L.A. food morality; it was survival. I lived on sticky rice and bean sprouts. Chewing felt like customer service.

After an uncomfortable amount of time sitting solo at the buffet, I spotted a young Chinese actress from the Vegas shoot and her mother. The seven-year-old girl spoke a little English; the mom, none. They planned a beach walk. I asked to join like a polite stray. The mother smiled and nodded. I wasn't sure if she understood me or was just trying to nod me off politely.

The gray sky hid the neon aqua water under clouds like it was the sea's nap time. We walked, spotted mini crabs scattering across the wet sand and collected shells. I couldn't tell if the mother and daughter had ever seen an ocean like this, or any ocean at all. Either way, the girl's giggles lightened the gravity in my chest. Novelty had started to feel like free fall. I needed a call sheet, a script, anything to prove I belonged.

After the beach walk, I found two English-speaking castmates I remembered from Vegas back at the buffet. We weren't close, but I still hugged them like cousins at a funeral. I needed familiar humans to break things down for me. They had arrived a few days prior and were put up at a resort fully equipped with A/C, a fridge, nightly entertainment and a beachfront pool. What the fuck? I gathered from them that my janky hotel housed day-players, and the resort held series regulars. It seemed that even my guest star expansion wasn't enough to spend resort money on me. The business of show business.

Also, staying at my shit palace hotel was Gabriel, a ridiculously charming

Brazilian I'd met once in Vegas. He reminded me of my Swedish uncle Tomas who embodied pure light and laughter and was everyone's favorite person. He never took life too seriously and that energy was infectious. Gabriel wore the same ease, the same joke-around-the-corner humor that made rooms exhale. I instantly felt comfortable with him.

My new bestie mentioned a sunrise at this spot he'd heard about on the other side of the island. He'd rented a car and was leaving around 4:30am the next morning.

"You want to come?" he tipped his chin toward the door, toothpick wagging in his smile like it was beckoning me.

The adventurer in me said yes before the question even landed. Then a shiver. Under the buzzing fluorescents in a buffet that smelled like fryer oil and damp carpet, humidity slicking the backs of our chairs, this tall, beautiful man so unapologetically himself was asking me out? Was I dreaming? Okay, maybe not asking me out on a date-date, but my stomach flipped like I was in high school, and my crush just performed his promposal in front of the whole school.

Gabriel towered over me, shoulders loose, stance easy, with the kind of presence that made a room feel smaller around him. I don't know when in my life this started, but I'd become highly skilled in clocking where people carried their center of gravity, almost the way some people notice shoes. Some people carried it in their heads like you could see the forehead tension, the way logic led the feet. That was Z, one hundred percent. All intellect. Others led with their hearts: soft chests, quick to mist over at commercials, always reading the room for who needed water. Then there were the grounded ones, weight dropped low, like their heels had roots. Garden keepers. Storm weatherers. Just earthy. And finally, the pelvis-led: not crass, just lit from the sacrum out. They moved from gut and heat, their sexual current entering a beat before they did. Those were always dangerous for me. I didn't just recognize them; I was them. And this was also Gabriel.

So there I was in that nasty buffet with Gabriel and Gabriel's crotch, which arrived half a step ahead of his body. Not because he wanted anyone to stare, but because that's where his life force lived and leaked. Maybe it was the Brazilian ease. Maybe he just knew he was sexy. Either way, he'd invited me on an adventure, and a choice planted itself between us.

My body said, fuck yes. My mind said, *So you're going to get in a car with a beautiful man you barely know in the dark and drive to a remote spot on an island you know nothing about with no cell service? This sounds like the opening of a very bad horror film. Or at least one where someone's clothes are coming off.*

I thought about Z. I felt like I was cheating on him just for being invited. I know, I know. I handled dicks all day for money, yet somehow this felt more dangerous. Is this allowed? Should I go out on an adventure with this gorgeous specimen? *Will I get in trouble just for having these thoughts? But the charm, the accent. What's a sexually repressed dick fixer supposed to do?*

Mind you, this all happened in about 30 seconds of him asking me to go. Shit was complex up there in my mind.

Gabriel looked at me for an answer. I squirmed in my chair at our stale and shitty buffet restaurant, my thighs sticking to the vinyl. I drew a breath that tasted like sweet-and-sour steam and remembered I was approaching nearly a year of losing my dad, a year of fixing dicks, and learning how to be safe around all kinds of men, even the attractive ones and even if the one I lived with still wouldn't fuck me.

The "you only live once" mindset screamed at me. I eventually thought: *Fuck it. I can handle this. I can be attracted to him and not beg him to rip my clothes off. Right?*

"Yeah, I'll go," I said nonchalantly, trying to sound cooler than my pulse.

"Great!" He smiled back.

I didn't sleep at all that first night in Saipan. Not with Gabriel's room sharing a wall with mine and the island air glued to my skin. The fan clacked like it had a limp. The bedspread was pure sandpaper, polyester bristle prickling my side every time I tried to turn over. I stared at the dark tacky walls and argued with myself: responsible me said, *Girl, this is how Dateline episodes start.* Feral me purred, *Or great stories.* At 4:17 a.m., a soft knock rattled the hollow door. I exhaled, slipped on my shoes, and chose the story.

We pulled away from the hotel while the island was still asleep. Headlights tunneled through mist; the wipers squeaked in a nervous rhythm. Gabriel missed a turn, then another. The road broke into ruts, and the car fishtailed, tires gulping mud like pudding. Tropical rain had lacquered everything: palm fronds, mile markers, my courage. Twice we rocked the car free, engine whining, and finally rolled into a dirt pullout that smelled like wet leaves and salt.

"Come on!"

Gabriel sprang from the driver's seat, and I followed, because of course I did. I didn't know where the hell I was and barely knew who the hell he was, but his fearless spirit tugged me forward like a rope.

We pushed into grass taller than me, and I'm nearly 5'6". Blades slapped my thighs; dew soaked my calves. The ground gave underfoot, spongy and treacherous, and the sky held on to that thick pre-dawn blue. No streetlights. No house lights. No moon. Just the ocean breathing somewhere ahead and our shoes sucking at the mud. "It's always darkest before dawn" stopped being a motivational poster and turned into a visibility report.

A thin seam of light finally stitched the horizon; the ocean took shape, pewter and endless. We weren't quite where Gabriel wanted to be. He slowed behind me, fishing for his phone.

"Stop!" he shouted.

I froze. Adrenaline spiked. What?

"That's a beautiful picture!"

He grinned, lifted his phone, and snapped one.

God, could he be cuter? Fucker.

I turned to keep going and my sandal slid. My toe met nothing. "Oh, shit!"

Air rushed past. Dirt from my shoe tumbled into a void that went down for days. Vertigo slammed me; the world tilted; my stomach tried to leave the chat. I flung myself backward on instinct, knees buckling.

Gabriel reached me in two strides, peered over the edge, cursed in Portuguese, then tipped his face up in a fast prayer.

"We made it, eh? That was close."

Yeah, Gabriel. That was fucking close. I nearly plummeted to my death! Jesus.

"You saved me," I managed, throat tight.

"No, your beauty did."

Okay, very smooth, bro. But also, don't. But also... Fuck!

Gabriel did save me or his compulsion to snap a photo of me did. Either way, it was a clean hit on my fear response and a memory branded in high-res. He was fearless and loose and stupid hot; I was none of those things in that second. I admired his risk-drunk spirit and swallowed the part where my stomach was still doing cartwheels.

My pulse came down just as the horizon lifted. Then the sun started its striptease and my nerves evaporated. The sky flipped palettes like it was auditioning, lavender to apricot to a punch of tangerine, each layer brighter than the last. The Pacific Ocean below us glittered like someone had dragged a cursor across it and cranked the saturation. My eyes stung. Tears, not wind.

Gratitude slammed into guilt. *Thank you for this. Why me, though? Why not Z? My mom? My sisters? My dad?* I'd already been handed so much good, at least at The Clinic, and here I was on a cliff inside a screensaver. It felt stolen. Like I'd cut the line and taken more handouts than a person needs.

But as the sun peeked over the horizon, the sound of the world rose with it. In the village below our cliff, the day was starting. One rooster crowed, then another answered. A dog barked. A scooter coughed to life. More roosters, more engines, a human cough, a screen door slam. The cacophony of daybreak in the village was like a soundtrack that proved life was there.

The sounds of community steadied me. I wasn't alone on this island; I was a visitor, yes. But people lived here, loved here, paid bills and washed dishes here. I was borrowing their morning. Maybe this wouldn't be a detour from my dick-fixing life so much as a refill. Maybe I'd be okay, even with a pointless crush, because Gabriel flew out later that day. Thank God. I did not need his sexy orbit tugging at me while he showered feet away from where I slept.

Also, why did the humidity there make me feral? Not like Cabo. In Saipan, with my joints oiled and skin dewy, heat in my body pooled low and insistent. Ripe and ready. *Beat it, Gabriel. Leave me and my tropical horniness alone.*

After a few days of polite pestering and full-contact producer wrangling, I talked my way into a room at the nice resort. Victory-ish. The only room left sat on the weather-beaten wing, where the trade winds played my doorframe like a flute. Gusts of wind knifed through the cracks, the lights hiccupped, and the Wi-Fi fainted whenever the palms started thrashing. Still, sheets that didn't smell like wet mop water felt like luxury. Progress.

Then came the work, or the absence of anything resembling it. No scripts. Twenty-hour shooting days. On-call seven days a week. No food or water on set. I'd get an hour's notice for work and a "Come now," text, then sit in a folding chair while departments wandered in circles. The shoot ran like a preschool without a teacher: lots of noise, sticky hands, and no one knew where their shoes were.

My phone refused an international SIM card, so the second I stepped off hotel

Wi-Fi I went mute. No calling Z. No easy lifeline to The Clinic. Training our new admin across the time zones meant midnight emails and 3 a.m. spreadsheets that wouldn't send. "Working remotely" turned into "survive the day and pray the router reboots by night."

By week's end, I'd worked one day. One scene. Familiar suspicion pricked the back of my neck. Was this Vegas déjà vu with better views and worse planning? There was no hopping home and back from here; the math didn't math. Had my "extended" role been a single pickup? I needed to get home. The situation wasn't just shaky, it was sinking.

Then came the money. A Chinese production assistant texted a hotel address and told me to bring receipts if I wanted to get paid my weekly rate. Okay. The hotel I met him at was dim and damp and the lobby carried that signature tropical blend of bleach and mold. He hustled me down a corridor with humming fluorescents and carpet that squished. He parked me outside a random hotel room door. A man slipped out without eye contact; my escort tipped his chin—go in.

Inside, a folding table sagged under neat bricks of cash and curling paper receipts. An older Chinese woman in a red visor sat beneath a buzzing light like a bingo queen moonlighting as a banker. She didn't greet me, just flicked two fingers at my envelope. I handed it over. She counted, thwick, thwick, thwick, like we were filming a music video and then pushed a stack across the table. Two thousand U.S. dollars. No bank. No signature. FDIC who?

What the hell was this underground cash-based mob shit? How was I supposed to keep this amount of money safe? I stuffed the cash in my bag, murmured thanks, and walked out feeling dazed and suddenly very robbable.

I texted the director: *What's next?*

"Hi Betty!" he replied, all ha-ha emojis. He loved calling me by my character's name, like a laugh track could soften chaos.

"They didn't tell you? You're not finished. You'll be here a while longer."

Wait, what?

"You said one week," I typed, pulse spiking.

"Ha! You know production. Weather is crazy. Lots of delays."

I did know production. I'd produced a feature that actually fed people and ran on schedules. This wasn't it. Heat rose in my throat, rage and jet lag doing shots.

"How much longer?" I snapped.

"I don't know. But you're in paradise. Enjoy it, Betty! This is what we worked for. Our dreams!"

I didn't need a perspective pep talk; I needed a plan. Structure. A date. A timeline. I had a clinic, clients, a dog with seizures, a partner already drowning back home. Then my stomach dropped as the missing puzzle piece clicked: they'd never booked me a return flight. One way in. No way out. At least not on their dime. Shit.

I'd been sent a one-way ticket: production's polite way of saying, "We have no idea when you're leaving." And I'd said yes. I got on the plane. Out there, I was on their clock, not mine. No longer the boss-bitch VP of Dicks. At The Clinic, I knew my days to the minute: gloves on, settings set, stories unfurling one client at a time. The only surprise I allowed was the first handshake with a new dick and the why behind its mutiny. On the island, I was just "talent," pinned to a call sheet the monsoon season weather ate for breakfast. Squalls slapped the palms sideways, tarps snapped like flags, and the sky rewrote the schedule every hour.

I wasn't in paradise. I was in purgatory. But God, it was gorgeous. So, I stayed.

The director wasn't wrong: getting paid to do the thing I loved was the point. There was no Plan B, no secret career I'd tucked away in case the dream didn't call back. The little girl who'd clung to the actor dream since age two; she deserved a turn on the ride.

But home didn't pause because I'd pressed play. The Clinic kept humming. Dicks kept breaking. Men kept showing up with shame heavy as wet wool, asking for a room where it could finally be set down. And Z... he was back in L.A., alone with our seizure-prone dog and a house of chores, carrying weight he never signed up for while I chased a dream he maybe never entirely believed would stick.

The dream was mine; the consequences were ours.

So there I stood on a borrowed island with salt drying on my lips, trade winds rattling the thin hotel windows, no return ticket in my inbox and zero control, feeling the truth rise like tidewater in my throat: if this trip didn't break me, it might break everything else.

CHAPTER 16
LOST ON DICK ISLAND

"The trick to surviving the unknown? Relax, release, and try not to think about your dick."

—100% me

One week on Saipan turned into two. Then three. Then four.

Each morning I woke to the same salt-sticky air and a phone screen with no answers from production. No call sheet, no script pages, just rumors riding the trade winds. I befriended one of the writers; even he looked confused, as if the humidity had melted the plot right off the whiteboard. The whole thing felt like a prank with better scenery. My brain chased logic; the island shrugged back.

By now, paparazzi swarmed our sets, trying to catch shots of the A-list Chinese mega stars headlining our highly anticipated TV show. The paps caught one of my scenes, and by sundown the photos surfaced in the Saipan local paper. There I was: "big Hollywood actor." I snorted, half mortified, half delighted. They were so very wrong, but why ruin the island's best fantasy since World War II? Let them have their A-listers. I found the article online, Wi-Fi stuttering like a bad heartbeat, and shot it off to my family the second the bars held steady. No one in the states knows who I am, but here? I was a celebrity. My family had to know and laugh with me. My sisters did not disappoint with their repeating lol emojis and gifs.

At some point, Jin, a Chinese actor with a wristwatch that ticked louder than his conscience, asked me to kayak the lagoon. Early in my stay, I kept my leash short: stay close enough to Wi-Fi in case I needed to sprint back if production suddenly remembered I existed, but I ventured far enough to taste the island. The idea of skimming that glassy turquoise bowl tugged at me. I said yes, measured. Enjoy the view, stay within earshot of chaos.

Jin was no Gabriel. He led with a flashy aura that screamed, "Look how privileged I am!" Cute, sure, but the arrogance dulled the shine. He hinted he came from money back in China and didn't need this show; he was "doing them a favor." (Later I learned his part was very small. You'd never know it from the way he strutted like the star, and the island owed him rent.)

Jin had rented the loudest car on Saipan and revved it like foreplay. "Hear that?" he shouted over the engine, waiting for me to melt. I smiled, filed it under Male Ego 101, and let it pass. He was at least five years younger than me and still naive enough to think horsepower equals charisma.

At the beach, he haggled with the kayak rental guys like we were at a flea market. His bartering felt performative, like he needed me to witness his business acumen. Poor thing. He had no idea who I was or what I did. I watched the show, saw straight through the smoke.

We pushed off into water so clear it looked backlit. Jin kept posing, snapping photos of me, then himself, then the two of us together like awkward honeymooners. The lagoon slapped gently against the hulls; sunscreen stung my eyes; everything smelled like salt and coconut.

Halfway across the lagoon, Jin's paddle clattered. His shoulders dropped, his breath labored. He wilted in the seat.

"You okay?" I muttered, knowing the answer. Men with egos that size don't go down easy, unless they're going down.

To my surprise Jin replied, "No. I can't breathe. I need help."

Wow. Good for you, sir. Finally, some authenticity.

"Call someone. Please." He pleaded, desperation overtaking his face.

"I got you." I paddled my way toward him.

"No, I need a boat or something." He insisted.

I gave Jin the courtesy of looking around at the empty lagoon. I looked at my phone. No bars.

"Sorry, man. I am the boat."

I bumped our kayaks together, threaded the rental rope through his bow handle, and cinched us tight. The knot burned my fingers; the current pushed back like a stubborn mule. Once Jin realized I was hauling him, he shrank into silence, his shame heavy as a third passenger. I dug in, back firing, blades biting. I paddled; he slumped. We inched toward shore.

Did I have much experience kayaking? Not at all. Did my rescuer complex love a test? Absolutely.

We slid up onto the sand, my arms like jelly, his pride in pieces. I didn't gloat. Not this time. Under the peacock feathers I'd seen the scared boy, ribcage fluttering like a trapped bird.

There, there, little one, I thought. Mama's here.

I could've mocked the panic, could've weaponized the story. But that wasn't me, and after a year of dick fixing, I knew too much about men to kick them where they hid. Add culture to the mix and I felt the weight of it: the traditional pride, the provider/protector script. Being towed in by a woman? That humiliation would leave a mark.

I never saw him again, or at least he made sure I didn't. Pride prefers distance. Losing face is easier when you avoid the witness.

Another night, a bunch of us actors drifted into a hole-in-the-wall dance club. Dancing had always been my first language; if a beat showed up, my body answered—on a treadmill, in produce aisles, mid-meeting with my agent—location and setting remained irrelevant. One trait straight from my father: the man loved a party.

The club wasn't much. Just a dim room, bass too hot for the speakers, and floors tacky enough to steal a high heel. But on this island, music felt like a gift. A release valve. That night the place swarmed with Navy guys, their ship docked for a quick turn. Most of my sunset photos already featured hulking silhouettes of tankers shouldering into the horizon like steel dinosaurs interrupting Eden. All I needed was a T-Rex and Jeff Goldblum whispering, "life finds a way," in my ear.

One sailor zeroed in on me. Let's call him Anthony. Or, judging by how a single rum-and-Coke turned his smile wobbly and his knees to Jell-O, Tipsy Tony. He was young and sweet, the kind of charming that only exists before life sands you down. His buzzed cheeks, high-and-tight fade, and heart on an unsecured channel broadcasted his naïveté across the room. The military wasn't my world, I hated guns and killing and war, but I led with curiosity. And after a year of dick fixing, I could spot a hairline crack in a heart from across a sticky dance floor.

A couple drinks in, Tipsy Tony's story unspooled. His wife was cheating while he'd been deployed; at least, that's what he said. His buddies, drunker and looser, filled in the parts he couldn't voice. Hurt. Embarrassment. Desperation. I felt it roll off him. Maybe I just missed my clients; I'd grown used to getting my daily dose of grief lobbed at me like dodgeballs in a middle-school gym. I needed my fix.

After I gave him my Clinic-honed, nonjudgmental listening, Tipsy Tony leaned in, shy and slurring. "Can we take a group picture? Like everyone." Then softer, just for me: "If you could stand next to me... it might make her jealous."

It took me a beat to clock it. Tipsy Tony wanted to use me; my face, my body, my presence—as bait. A pawn in a toxic marriage.

I considered saying no. I had every right to. But the tremor in his voice, the way he looked at me like I might patch his dignity for five seconds, I couldn't be cold. Not to this one. Did I mention I missed my clients?

We posed shoulder-to-shoulder in the group; someone snapped the photo. Tipsy Tony sent it off immediately.

Minutes later, his phone rang. His wife's voice tore through the tiny speaker, loud enough to turn heads. Tipsy Tony folded onto a barstool, phone pressed to his ear, face emptied out. Tears gathered. Sweat beaded and ran, shame opening every pore.

Did I help him or pour gasoline on a fire? I don't know. Mostly, I felt sorry. Sorry that boys are taught to fight for love with performance and power plays. Sorry that this kid had crossed an ocean to serve and came home discarded. Sorry that he measured his worth by whether he could spark jealousy in someone who'd already checked out. And sorriest that I knew this script too well.

He was Jack from The Clinic, begging his wife to see him. Or maybe even my dad. Same ache, different uniform.

Again, I saw how fragile men can be and how hungry they are to be chosen, to be seen. Even if they have to borrow someone else's face to prove they still matter to the person they love.

Meanwhile, I barely had contact with Z on the island, and I doubt that felt great on his end. Some of it was logistics, but some of it was the strange relief of not performing that I missed him. I didn't. And the honesty of that sat in my gut like a stone.

I pinged The Clinic whenever I had anything concrete about my return. Updates leaked through spotty Wi-Fi like rain through a tin roof, only when the storms didn't knock the power out. Every night a "goodnight" text from Z blinked onto my phone. If nothing else, the man was consistent over text. Seventeen hours ahead, I'd be mid-shoot or halfway to some jungle cove, then stumble back to a signal and find his bubbles waiting. Sometimes I answered. Sometimes I didn't. It was inconvenient for him and, embarrassingly, convenient for me.

Weeks of production company moves all over the island turned Saipan into a field guide: velvet-green ridgelines, cliffs gnawed by turquoise, beaches so bright they hurt your eyes. Saipan stayed small and simple and gorgeous, like a diorama come to life.

Tourists swarmed, mostly from China, renting neon-pink Mustangs and staging operatic poses against the neon green hills for their feeds. Taxis became a game of charades; most drivers didn't speak English, so I rode shotgun with my bilingual castmates directing from the back when I could. Otherwise a giant van scooped me up, piloted by a silent PA who didn't share a word with me. Being ferried through switchbacks by someone I couldn't speak to felt like a new sport: surrendering my faith in the universe, one blind curve at a time.

The production flew in dozens of Russian actors to play "Americans." The cinematographers cheated Saipan's cliffs for the mountains of Las Vegas, then realized they needed white faces to sell the illusion. Chinese PAs trolled the island in vans, flagging down any pale tourist with a pulse. They even tried to recruit me once, not realizing I was already cast. Subtlety wasn't the brief. They needed bodies.

A couple of the "Americans" turned out to be actual Russian locals who'd washed up on Saipan years ago. No experience, but they were white, box checked, so the show bumped them to featured extras. I never got the full story of what called them to this speck of Pacific, but they were generous as hell, eager to show me and a few castmates their secret corners of the island as they rarely got tourists they could bond with.

It took a couple of weeks before I let myself enjoy any of the island.

Not knowing my wrap date kept me half-packed, half-guilty, tugged back toward The Clinic like I'd snuck out of work, and the bell was about to ring. I told myself I wasn't allowed to have fun while living a double life. I couldn't admit the freedom felt... good. But my castmates wanted to roam, and the Russians, delighted to play tour guide, started us slow: a small boat to a thumbprint of an islet you can circumnavigate in under an hour. We walked a lace of shoreline, crab claws clicking like china, pockets of shells winking in the foam. Stray dogs trailed us, ribs like xylophones, every single one begging for the role of "dog I adopt against my better judgment." The place felt slightly off-planet, same sky, different rules.

I started to relax around the men on the island. We saw each other on set, then again between call times; mud on our shoes, sand in our socks, swapping snacks and stories. I let the curtain drop about my other life. "Back home I fix dicks," I said, as casually as if I'd said "taxes." Brakes squealed. Eyes widened. Then the jokes rolled in, same as they did with my friends in L.A.

"Think mine's okay? Would you... you know... check it?"

By then I could conduct the male ego like a symphony. I knew they were kidding and also fishing. A yes would hit the vein of whatever insecurity hummed beneath the banter. I stuck to my line. "Buy a pump. Maintenance, not triage. Even if you're fine now, you won't be forever. Pumps add years to the life of your dick." They laughed like I'd told a bit, but I watched them tuck the advice away for later.

Somewhere in week four, I felt a shift. My body clicked into island mode. I'd bushwhacked through jungle so green it made paint jealous, nearly slipped to my death on rainy hiking paths, kayaked through shark infested waters, and scaled rocks with crabs the size of my torso. I said yes to everything. The tightrope between control and surrender went slack; I stopped white-knuckling the future. I chased the next jolt and, to my surprise, didn't miss home at all.

Then the Russians "knew a guy who knew a guy," and suddenly a few of us were climbing into a bright red helicopter for free. I'd never flown in a helicopter before. The rotors thumped a heartbeat through my ribs; the headset hissed; hot diesel and sea salt braided in the air. We lifted and the island unrolled like a green rug: knife-bright cliffs, sugar-pale crescents of beach untouched by footprints, a Japanese war plane sleeping on the bay floor like a myth you could point to. On the roads below, neon-pink Mustangs dotted the jungle like spilled candy, tourists staging their feeds against the hills. Hanging in that open-air cradle, I felt the island ask me to stop, just for a breath, and take it all in at once.

By then, fear loosened its grip and gratitude took its place. I kept looking around like, *how is this my life?* The guilt played on loop, Groundhog Day in my chest, while, like the movie, the resort lobby piped the same tinny island song every morning and, outside those sliding doors, a brand-new adventure clocked in for work.

The rhythm on the island threw my life at The Clinic into sharp focus. Back home I logged ten and twelve-hour days, patching other people's pain, absorbing storm systems that weren't mine. It was meaningful, sure, but it wasn't me. This feral freedom, this island version of myself with sea salt in my hair and sky in my lungs, felt truer than anything I'd ever lived.

I slicked coconut oil for sunscreen and watched fifteen pounds melt off because "vegan" on Saipan translated to "good luck." I strutted through rainstorms along the island roads while wild cows grazed the verge. Thai massages were twenty bucks; I got them like vitamins, except my favorite masseuse was narcoleptic and would doze off mid-stroke. I'd give a little shimmy, she'd wake, and we'd carry on. It felt weirdly on brand for Saipan. The island slowed us all down.

A couple times, I'd be mid-kayak in open water when a text pinged: You're up. I'd sprint to the Russians' car, shimmy out of wet clothes in the backseat, do my makeup in a side mirror, brush sand off my calves, and dive into wardrobe. A PA would slap sides into my hand – two-page brand-new monologues, surprise! There was no time to prep, no time to spiral. Just hit your mark and breathe. Just flowing in the moment. Just now.

I also made a friend: Wella, my hotel housekeeper, a beautiful trans woman from a tiny Philippine island with a laugh that filled the hallway. She had intel on every room. Who left food in the sheets (Koreans), who lived so clean, it's like they didn't exist (Japanese), who treated the place like a gas station bathroom (Chinese). She monologued and I listened, fascinated by her experience. She was saving to open a drinking-water shop back home, and she liked me because I didn't make her work harder than she had to; I kept my space tidy. Most days she just popped in with fresh towels and fresher gossip.

One night a handful of us actors got tapped to dine with city officials at the island's casino, the place where, I realized, the money changed hands. The building looked fresh-poured and over polished, Saipan's best imitation of Vegas: mirrored columns, blue-neon veins, chandeliers trying a little too hard. But the tourists weren't global; they were almost exclusively Chinese, drifting between baccarat tables and high-limit rooms like schools of glittering fish.

They funneled us to a banquet hall in the back and parked us around a lacquered round table big enough to land a drone on. The mayor of Saipan sat there, plus a cluster of people who wore importance like a boutonnière. Servers multiplied at our elbows, laying down course after mysterious course I couldn't identify, much less eat. I kept my smile fixed and my teacup full.

For every sip, a fresh pour appeared. It was ceremonial, relentless, a tide.

An official clocked my untouched plates. "You only like tea?" he asked, smiling.

"Oh, no. I'm vegan," I said, still lifting the cup.

His confusion hung for a beat. A castmate leaned in and smoothed it over in Mandarin: "She's on a diet."

The official nodded, verdict delivered. "Actress. Always on diet."

I smiled back. Sure, sir. *Let's go with that stereotype.*

"This tea is for diet," he added, approving. "Very, very expensive, but good for you."

I angled toward another man for a translation of "expensive." He chuckled. "Pu-erh. Around ten thousand U.S. dollars per pot."

I nearly baptized the table in a spit take. I was, no exaggeration, on cup number twelve. Nervous-me is a fidgeter. I chew ice, shred napkins, apparently mainline five-figure tea so I don't blurt something that pegs me as the loud, ignorant American.

"Are you serious?" I whispered, horrified.

"Yeah. Look it up," he barked, amused.

I did. He was right. Shit balls. Some Pu-erh tea really does fetch the price of a used car. No one said a word as I kept sipping. They simply let me drink the rare leaves like tap water. I went back to the resort that night equal parts mortified and caffeinated, and, fine, I swear I woke up ten pounds lighter. If nothing else, the tea was... effective.

Shedding the weight—okay, the shame—of that tea fiasco loosened something else I'd been hauling around: the heaviness of home I kept refusing to look at. I chose, deliberately, to be present on this island I didn't understand. I was fully there. Immersed. Willing to learn. I'd even implemented using the indigenous Chamorro language greeting "Hafa adai" (hah-fuh-day), which meant "hello".

So when production offered a few of us a chance to skydive, my mouth said yes before my brain could file an objection. Then, of course, panic sprinted in. I'd never jumped out of a damn plane before! I'd always been loudly anti "plummet toward earth for fun." My imagination was a 4D horror theater; it screened outcomes, not rewards.

The Skydive Saipan folks wanted us there before sunrise, the first flight of the day. It had poured all night, and the rain still needled the windows at 4 a.m. I stared into the wet dark and muttered, "No way this is happening." I climbed into the transport van with my castmates and the Russians anyway.

"This is getting canceled, right?" I asked, bargaining.

"The weather changes every thirty minutes here. We'll be fine," one of the Russians shrugged me off, as if forecasting was a hobby.

That nonchalant response came from the guy rumored to be ex-KGB, who owned at least twelve guns, and who'd already dragged me to a shooting range "for research." "If you're playing a cop with a prop," he'd said, "you should know how a real one kicks." He wasn't wrong. My gun aversion had kept that line on my acting résumé pure fiction. On Saipan, there were no such lines. I shot handguns, semi-automatics, automatics, guns with names I couldn't remember, weights my wrists would never forget. Big. Loud. Heavy. Terrifying. The kind of thunder that echoes in your skeleton.

We reached the drop zone in the island's belly while the sky remained black. Sodium lights buzzed. Mud sucked at our shoes. They sat us in front of a grainy training video; smiling tandem pairs, a cartoon parachute blossoming like a miracle, then zipped us into suits that smelled like adrenaline and disinfectant. The rain thinned to a drizzle, but my certainty didn't: either I would die here for agreeing to this, or... no, my brain refused to write a second option. Stress hormones ran the show.

Then I met my guy, Marcel, the Frenchman I would let strap me to his chest so we could trust our lives to a square of fabric and some cords together. Harness in his hands, grin on his face.

Honestly, what the hell was I thinking?

"You like your life, right?" I blurted, skipping introductions.

"Of course," he said, French accent curling around the words.

"Good. So you've got a wife, kids, plants you water. People who need you around. And you've done this before?" My laugh came out high and feral.

He found my terror adorable. "Only once, a long time ago. But I think I remember how."

Not the time for jokes, Marcel!

Yet his humor matched mine like a mirror. I gave him points for his wit and charm.

We waddled outside, strapped together, as the sky unzipped. Clouds thinned and pinked at the edges. They loaded us by weight: heavier guys first, me last. Fantastic.

"Smile, Kristina" he grinned through his perfect French teeth. He wore cameras like jewelry; helmet, chest, wrist—every angle ready.

"Oh, God. We're filming this? You're documenting my death?" I choked out, not amused.

Fine, Marcel. I'll smile because I always laugh when I'm in pain. That's my brand.

The plane clawed into the air. We climbed above a quilt of cloud, the sun rising, rain downgrading to a mist. Two by two, my castmates and their tandem partners vanished into the blue. *Fuck!* Then it was our turn. *Double Fuck!*

Marcel inched us to the hatch. I was harnessed to him like a front-pack baby; my legs dangled over the island that had somehow adopted me. My heart pounded at my chest cavity, trying to escape.

"Ready?" he shouted into my ear.

Hell no!

"Marcel! You and I are married now. My life is in your hands. Please don't—"

He launched us.

Oh, shit.

Wind punched open my mouth and flooded my nose. The world blurred into speed. Then, snap, the chute yanked us upright and—BOOM.

Stillness.

Rainbows rimmed the horizon like parentheses. Below, Saipan and her sister islands, green spines, white cuffs of beach, water so turquoise it looked photoshopped, everything soaked in sunrise. The light kept repainting everything: jade cliffs, lacquered ocean, the island's pulse. This wasn't a YouTube drone shot. It was right there, obliterating the border between me and it until I wasn't sure where I ended.

I thought of my dad. My mom. Everyone I'd ever loved. *Why me? Why this?* The old loop started: *I don't deserve this.* The same script I ran with money, love, time, my body. *I'm not a keeper of good things; I'm a conduit. Pass it through, don't hold. This joy doesn't belong to me. This freedom is too good for me. So why do I feel it?*

My tears evaporated midair. We drifted to earth and skidded a clumsy landing.

"Marcel," I said, breathless. "We are definitely married now. You and me. Forever. We're sky-married."

He laughed. We divorced seconds later on the grass, but I felt indebted to him anyway. Maybe it was just his job. To me, it was a permanent memory stapled to my soul.

I rode the skydiving high, adrenaline fizzing in my veins, euphoria humming under my skin. Spared again. Not the first time I'd felt like I'd slipped past some cosmic bouncer and avoided my inevitable demise. I carried the rush straight to set and shoved it in a mental locker. Work hat on. Back to being Betty, the cop chasing bad guys in a plot I still couldn't map, holster digging into my hip, powdery dust settling on my boots while a PA yelled for last looks.

All that beauty and dumb luck around me cracked something open. I started posting photos on Instagram for the first time in my adult life. I didn't even know how IG worked. A castmate had to show me how to crop a square and pick a filter without making my face look like a laminated menu. I'd never wanted the world to see my day job. Dick fixer felt too weird to explain and my shame kept a hand over the lens. But this? This I wanted witnessed. The actor. The artist. The skydiver. The woman doing what she'd promised L.A. upon arrival eleven years earlier. She did it. She had a new title working as an international actor. She felt air in her lungs. She felt worthy.

For the first time, I felt proud enough to be seen. Not hiding until I hit some mythical benchmark. Not apologizing for joy I hadn't "earned." Just visible.

But the island didn't only hand me freedom; it handed me quiet. In the quiet, feelings queued up like planes on a runway. Night after night, power flickered, the ceiling fan slowed, the ocean inhaled and exhaled against the reef, and the stillness pressed its palm to my chest. No clients. No clinic. No errands disguised as purpose. Just me. And inside that hush, the one feeling I kept outrunning raised its hand.

Grief.

CHAPTER 17
OFF THE DICK DEEP END

"You can't cross the sea merely by standing and staring at your dick."

—inspired by Rabindranath Tagore

The one-year anniversary of my father's death pressed closer like a storm building offshore. Paradise didn't blunt it. Even on this beautiful island, even with all the exciting adventure and my newfound liberation of living in the moment, I couldn't escape the dread of facing one year without him. And when the power snapped off at night, as it often did, the island handed me silence on a silver platter. My tiny hotel room filled with wet heat and the pitter patter of geckos on plaster. I didn't drink. I didn't take drugs. I didn't even have an island boy crush to pin to my daydreams. I wasn't tired enough to sleep, so I just sat there soaked in the sorrow. With him.

One night I walked down to the hotel beach alone to see the full moon. The damp sand squeaked under my toes; the ocean hissed like it was ironing the shore flat. "Moon" was apparently my first word. According to my dad, I'd sat on his shoulders, a chubby finger stabbing the sky while my mouth struggled to form the word. He told that story forever, like it proved something holy about us. And because of that story, he'd anointed himself as the man in the moon to me. The cosmic night-light after I left home at 18; proof there was a father-shaped guardian posted in the heavens watching over me.

But tonight the moon felt vacant. No man. No guardian. Just light on dark, heavy water.

I stood in the surf and counted what he'd never know about me—this wild year I'd survived, the famous dicks I'd coaxed back to life, the ridiculous fact that his daughter was a TV star in China, the husband he'd never meet, the children he'd never hold. The moon carved a silver road across the black Pacific, and I stared up into it, throat raw.

Fuck you, Dad.

The tears hit hard. I felt abandoned all over again. Alone. My mom was alone. My sisters were alone. All his girls, the leftovers of his legacy cut short. The loneliness gutted me. The man who was supposed to protect and provide, the man we were meant to fall back on, was gone. And the sting inside the sting: he'd been gone long before he died. But at least when he was alive, there was still a chance he might show up. Even his non-participating, inconsistent presence soothed me more than this silence did. More than a dead dad.

I sank into the sand and rewound the whole losing-him reel. The first time I ever felt truly safe with my dad, as insane as it sounds, was the day I learned he had cancer.

The call came from him. Not my mom. Not one of my sisters. Him.

"Dad" lit up on my phone and dread went straight to my gut, cold and lead-heavy.

Someone died. Had to be. Mom? One of my sisters? All of them? Bob Denton didn't call. Ever. If he was dialing, the news had edges.

I was driving. L.A. gridlock had welded the 101 into a red river of brake lights. Typically, I rejected calls at home; in traffic, I'd answer bullshit spam to numb the crawl. But my father calling with bad news? I wasn't sure I could handle it.

I panicked and answered anyway. Ripped the band-aide off.

"Hey, babe..." His voice was soft. Sullen. Gentle.

Something was very, very wrong.

"I'm calling to let you know some bad news."

I fucking knew it! Just say it. My heart cannot beat any faster without leaving.

"I'm sick."

Sick? The invincible Bob Denton? Sick like a cold? Okay?

I could hear my mom muttering in the background. I still wondered why he was calling and not her. I talked about him on the phone, not to him.

He kept going: prostate cancer.

Cancer. The not-fun, not-cheeky, not-funny C-word. I knew fuck-all about cancer at the time. Not the types, stages, the fucked-up scale from

"Eh, they'll just remove it," to "You're absolutely fucked." Nobody close to me had been diagnosed with cancer, so it was just a shadow word I understood only as bad.

Then the details dropped: usually prostate cancer is treatable. Most men live. But they caught his late. Too late. It had already spread. To his liver. To his spine. Stage four. Terminal. They gave him two to three years to live.

Two to three years? To live? On Earth? What the fuck? And who the fuck are "they"?

The words pinged around the car like loose screws. None of my father's Shakespearean level tragedy of a monologue computed. All I really heard was "terminal cancer," and the rest of me liquefied. I came apart in the driver's seat, ugly sobbing in a sea of Teslas and Priuses, the dashboard blinking calmly while my world tilted.

My dad delivered the facts like a script he'd already run in the mirror. Knowing him, he had. He'd always been a storyteller; I was surely the last stop on his call sheet after my sisters, my aunt, maybe his closest friends. The speech already worn smooth from repetition.

The curse of being the only kid who moved away: you learn everything last.

After that, nothing landed. His words turned to radio snow. I sat in a sea of brake lights, fingers welded to the steering wheel, and sobbed an ugly, hiccupping, shoulder-shaking cry while a horn orchestra blared around me.

Then he did something he had never done in my entire life: he comforted me.

His voice softened. He stayed with me. He told me he was okay, strangely at peace with the diagnosis. He'd started a bucket list. He was going to make the most of what time he had left. And he promised he'd be there for me. Until the end.

The fuck?

It wasn't just his words; it was the way he said them. No venom. No jabs. No shrugging detachment. No sarcastic little knives. Just presence. And I had no file folder for that.

This motherfucker has been capable of gentleness all along? Now he knows how to be a father? Now he wants to show up like this? Now – after he finds out he's dying?

Rage flared inside me. Too late for tenderness.

And yet there it was: a calm, grounded version of my dad, death softening his edges into someone I almost recognized. The timing felt like a joke I couldn't laugh at, just madness.

I hated how safe I suddenly felt, how seen by the man who'd taught me men could not be trusted. My insides misfired: confusion buzzing under my skin, and under the confusion, fear, chest compressing, breath-thinning fear. For him. For my mom. For the shape of this cancer.

Would it hurt? Would he suffer? Would I?

I stared through the windshield, at the freeway of fellow L.A. commuters. A thousand thoughts ricocheted; jagged feelings leaked out my eyes and carved salty tracks down my cheeks while I tried to breathe around the lump in my throat.

I don't remember how the call ended. I do remember I had fancy lunch plans my Google Maps app was dragging my car toward. Lunch on the fancy Westside of L.A., where they Botox the forehead to bury the feelings; where emotion belongs in a dark theater, not under a Michelin star.

My lunch dates were friends who were also former bosses, people I deeply adored and low-key feared disappointing. With them, I usually showed up lacquered and buoyant: polished, charming, unbothered, the woman who chirps, "I'm great, thanks!" Even when my bank was sending me *low account balance* notification texts.

Five minutes into the meal I couldn't hold the mask. Panic and grief choked my throat. The terror of what was coming for my father and my family shrank the room.

"I'm sorry, you guys," I blurted. "I just found out my dad has terminal cancer."

The voice wasn't mine. It sounded like a line reading I'd flubbed in a play, dropped into the wrong scene. The words clawed their way out and thudded onto the white linen like silverware slipping off a plate. I hadn't processed any of it; it didn't feel like my story yet. And still I said it, stamped finished.

My friends were perfect; kind, present, soft-eyed, the exact humans you'd want in a moment like that. And I hated their empathy. Not them, me. I didn't know how to be held without feeling pitied. I didn't know how to accept care without shrinking, without translating tenderness as weakness.

Somewhere in my fucked-up, codependent schooling, the kind you get from weathering other people's moods like storms, I learned that being cared for was dangerous. Care had strings. Comfort carried a bill. My job was to be the strong one, the funny one, the rock. Let someone take care of me? That felt like the ultimate humiliation, like handing over my spine.

And yet here I was with a story I hadn't ordered: Daughter of a dying man. A brand-new identity I had to figure out how to carry without dropping my own heart on the sidewalk.

I saw it happen almost instantly when I said the words out loud: faces flinched, shoulders cinched, sentences fell apart. People winced, shrank, fumbled. And then I did what I'd been trained to do since childhood; I cleaned up their discomfort for them. I smoothed the edges of my suffering so they wouldn't have to. Performed that I had already processed the gut punch. I shrank my grief to fit inside their comfort zone and made it sound like I was fine so they could stay fine. I took their discomfort like a hot plate and kept passing it to myself.

I left that lunch knowing something had cracked. I couldn't go back to the girl I'd been before the call. I couldn't unknow that the man I'd avoided, feared, and resented was... dying. My family had a countdown now. I had a deadline for forgiveness. A window to sort my shit before it slammed shut.

Overnight, I had to be my father's daughter again. Handle him like fine china. Be the good one, the steady one, the translator of everyone else's feelings. And somehow, despite a lifetime of his absence and digs and drunken spirals, he got to exit as the hero. Ain't that a bitch? The man who never intentionally cared for himself, who smoked and drank himself to sleep, received the one diagnosis that terrifies the world and became an instant saint. Poor fucking Bob. The double standard made me equal parts bitter and terrified.

I called my oncologist friend the minute I got home from lunch. He picked up on the first ring, the way doctor friends do when they can hear the quake in your hello. I laid out the basics: my dad, prostate cancer, stage four; liver, spine; terminal.

My friend went quiet for a beat and then lobbed the most brutal question I hadn't dared touch:

"How badly does your dad want to live?"

My heart dropped clear through my shoes. I knew the answer before he finished the sentence. My dad didn't.

He didn't really want to live—not enough to fight cancer. Not enough to overhaul the habits that had been eating him, or to soften into our family in a way that might make the last stretch count. He sounded resigned, maybe even peaceful, but not committed to staying. That truth hit harder than the diagnosis. If he didn't want to be here, nothing I did could anchor him. Not my manic research, not a color-coded protocol of miracle diets and alternative treatments. I hated how powerless I was. I couldn't script-doctor this story.

For once in my life, I couldn't perform my way out of pain. I couldn't earn my dad's love or out-hustle his fate. I had to unclench and let him go.

Gut-wrenching memories flooded me that night on that bright spec of an island in the Pacific, and I came apart. Like fully. I couldn't bolt, couldn't stuff the ache with work or dicks. I let the complicated fuckery of losing my difficult father land – bare, undisguised, no spin. Years of tension unspooled; anger and grief rattled loose and bled into the black water. The moon held the scene while the tide kept my secrets. Even the crusty little crabs gave me a wide berth, skittering around my meltdown like they feared splash damage. No one wanted to end up collateral in my emotional airstrike.

A few days later, a bunch of us island strays went to see the reboot of *A Star Is Born*. I only knew the Barbra Streisand version in broad strokes. My dad and my dance teacher worshiped her, so I did too. But this version had Bradley Cooper and Lady Gaga, two of my personal artist icons. As the story unfurled of a singer scraping rent together and still chasing her dreams, salted tears stiffened into my unwashed hair. When Cooper's character handed Gaga a chance to sing on stage and she let "Shallow" rip, I sobbed. Loud. Messy.

I cried for her. I cried for me. I cried for my dad.

That moment was every artist's fever dream. When someone points you to stage and says, Go. Show them who you are. To be seen. To be heard. To have what you love confirmed as worthy. And there I was, on a speck of island in the middle of nowhere, filming a bonkers Chinese TV series and getting my own moment. My dad never got his. He tried, sure. Karaoke at home, golfing in tournaments that didn't cost him anything too big. Big fish in the small pond. His safe zone. But it wasn't the same.

Once, sloppy in a drunken haze he told me, "I want to be you when I grow up."

What the fuck, dad?

I hated him for saying that. I thought it was pathetic.

You're the dad. I'm supposed to look up to you. You set the bar. You lead. Don't put that on me.

But walking out of the theater, I finally understood. He saw in me the thing he never had the courage to become. Maybe, in his backward, busted way, he was proud. Maybe he loved me the only way he knew how, by shoving a mic or a golf club into my hands and asking me to share his dream. If I, his firstborn, stamped him with approval the way his parents never had, maybe he could feel worthy of it.

And right then, I realized I was the one in the arena. I was the one playing. Heart open, spirit raw. Even if the show never aired in the U.S., even if no one back home saw a frame on TV, I'd done it. Like my castmate said in the makeup trailer after one brutal day filming in Vegas, "We're living somebody's dream." I was finally living mine.

The *A Star Is Born* soundtrack became the island's pulse during my stay; serenaded my grief at night, beckoned me into my awakening by dawn. I'd finally leapt off the deep end and hit water, not rock. Out there, the unknown stopped feeling like a threat and started feeling like oxygen. Every day tossed me a new dare, and I got so fluent in uncertainty that I forgot about the life waiting on my doorstep: the dick-fixin', special-needs dog-mom, sexless routine I'd built and accepted back home.

I wasn't the woman who'd landed on Saipan with a clenched jaw and a color-coded calendar. I went wild in the best way; unpredictable, untamed, ready to say yes before the universe finished its sentence. Schedules bored me. Plans felt like cages. I lived in the present tense and, for the first time in my life, felt free.

Still, freedom came with its tax. I missed one of my best friend's weddings and it pinched hard. But the island had an assignment for me. Something new was emerging. It was dragging me, messy and miraculously back home to myself.

By the end of my time on the island, I understood my dad more than ever. I'd let the pain of losing him move through me and become my teacher. And the pain professor showed me something I couldn't see before. My dad responsibly brought home paychecks, kept the lights on and then, in his spare time he chased his bliss. Golf. Heineken beer. Sinatra at full blast. He did what he wanted, how he wanted and when he wanted. Maybe he'd known the secret all along: feed your joy to keep the wolves of pain at the door. Maybe that's how he survived himself and protected us from his dark side. *Damn, dad. I get it.*

I felt my own anger loosen its teeth. His pain. Mine. I had to stop carrying both.

Finally, my scenes wrapped. One "quick" week across an ocean had shape-shifted into six full weeks on a postage-stamp island, and now they were shipping me home. Except... one more day called. My Russian friend had a Tinian adventure planned, and I needed it like a last cigarette before sobriety. The production had already booked my flight back to L.A., but I begged the coordinator to change it and slapped a bit of my own (potentially money-laundered) cash down for the difference. I wanted one more dawn of the fantasy. One more day to live the dream and delay the grind I'd once mistaken for fulfillment.

The airline moved the ticket; the production clutched its wallet and wouldn't cover my hotel room extension. Cheap bastards. A castmate tossed me a couch, and once again I was saved by two things that never failed me on this island: luck and kindness.

The next morning we hit the tiny Saipan airport and climbed into a six-seater island hopper with seats like lawn chairs and dreams bigger than its propellers. People commute between Tinian and Saipan on this little plane every day, which blew my mind. The engine rattled, it wheezed, it looked retired from service in 1983, and I still felt steady.

I'd already proved I wasn't scared of risky things anymore. I was all in, living immersed, protected by this weird new faith that it would all work out. My default had become yes. Fully surrendered to the universe.

We landed on Tinian and snagged the only rental car the airport had. A compact, paint-peeling, smelling faintly of wet rope little hatchback. Locals murmured that most folks had already cleared out of the island. "We gotta typhoon comin' tomorrow." A typhoon? Like a hurricane with a different outfit? I'd never lived anywhere that got either, so I didn't know what "storm" meant here. But the island did: everything went hushed. Air like glass. Palms holding their breath. The cliché struck me; there really was a calm before the storm.

We wound our way to the sites where the two atomic bombs were stored and launched in World War II. History books turned to hot concrete under my sandals. The placards were tidy; the ground felt haunted. We peered into caves where Japanese soldiers once hid, escape tunnels cut into coral. The air went dense and wrong in my lungs. Paradise was underlaid with something eerie and inhuman here. How does an island this tender carry that kind of scar?

Then we hit Taga Beach. The most beautiful stretch I'd seen my entire time there. It wasn't a beach so much as a cathedral of water: turquoise stained-glass shallows, chalk-white aisles of sand, cliffs for pews. A Blue Flag beach, they said; an international stamp that the water and shore meet the highest environmental standards. Pristine. Safe. It looked photoshopped by God.

At the far edge: a fifteen-foot cliff into a bowl of crystal water. Past-me wouldn't have gone near it. Sharks live here; I'm a guest. That's the shark's house. Also, I lack fins and gills. I am built for land. Too much unknown. Too much "what if."

Adult me had collected so many reasons to stay on the ledge. Kid me didn't. As a child I boogie-boarded and bodysurfed the murky bite of Santa Cruz, California waters like a seal pup with a death wish, no fear at all. Only later did I learn Santa Cruz hosts one of the highest concentrations of great whites. (Cue the Jaws theme music. I hear it, too.) But back then? Ignorance was oxygen. Those were some of the best hours of my childhood; salt in my hair, sand in my ears, daring the next wave and laughing when it slammed me.

Now, I wasn't ignorant of the risks of open-water swimming. I did the math. I'd let fear drive for years; But now, on this island, I yanked the wheel back. It wasn't time to be afraid anymore. It was time to step into the unknown and do it anyway.

So I jumped off the cliff. Like Lady Gaga, I went off the deep end and didn't meet the ground. Then I climbed back up and did it again. And again. We cheered, we belly-laughed, we wrung every last drop from the day. As the sun slid down and gold glazed the water, I knew the dream was ending. The island had rewired me, forever changed.

I didn't even cry that last day. I was too full. Too grateful. This place had cracked something sacred open in my soul. I'd never logged more sun, more salt, more hours with strangers who'd become family. I'd never been wilder or freer. The tightrope I'd walked—perfect daughter, perfect employee, best student, compliant and loyal girlfriend—snapped. I swan-dove into crystal-blue water and didn't look back.

Except I had to—less than 24 hours to go now. Reality marched toward me with its clipboard and schedule. I refused to flinch. I stayed in my body, in the moment.

My friend came running up to me at the beach, giggling, palms cupped. "Close your eyes." I did. He set something small and warm into my hand.

"Okay. You can look," he said, vibrating with pride.

I opened my eyes, and there it was: a Dick Rock. A smooth little stone perfectly sculpted by surf into one shaft and two testicles. Zero ambiguity. The universe, with her filthy sense of humor, had delivered.

He beamed. "Do you see it?"

I laughed because—oh, I saw it. In that ridiculous rock I saw a souvenir of the woman I'd been before this place, a token from the life I didn't know how to return to but knew I must. It was the perfect find at the perfect time, better than any trinket on a spinning rack. No gift shop could touch the Dick Rock. Thank you, Tinian.

We left Tinian under a sherbet sky and caught the last island hopper back to Saipan. I had an early flight to Hong Kong, but I rinsed the salt from my hair, pulled on clean clothes, and hustled to our weekend bar to say goodbye. A live band played and waved us up to sing. I'd never fronted a band, but I had to try. Of course I asked for "Black Velvet." I sang for my father, for the island, for this new iteration of me. I wasn't the woman who'd arrived. I was a spiritually awake creature who'd tasted pain and pleasure and found a new current of feminine power. Like sand carving stone into a dick, there was no undoing it.

The next morning, I took the first flight out. Walking up the jet bridge felt like handing over an organ I couldn't live without. I left Saipan and the cabin swallowed me; recycled air, plastic lemon, the thrum of engines that vibrated straight into my bones. I felt gutted, hollowed out, and not with the delicious uncertainty I'd learned to love there. This was the kind that keeps you chewing your nails and bargaining with your own brain at 3 a.m. The whole flight, my thoughts scored themselves to a villain's soundtrack; low, ominous, relentless. It felt like I was flying back into hell.

An eight-hour layover in Hong Kong gave me one last hit of wonder. I ran through the city like I was trying to win a scavenger hunt: neon stacked on neon, humid air sticking to my skin, glass towers knifing up from jungle-green mountains, the ocean flashing between them like a dare. It looked like someone had taken Manhattan and wedged it into a tropical mountain paradise on the sea. People from everywhere poured through the streets of this mega metropolis. It was electric, disorienting, diverse, beautiful and I drank it in like a final refill before last call.

After hours of chasing light and noise, I made it back to the airport and boarded the red-eye to L.A. A strange calm slid over me in the boarding line—pure gratitude rinsing me clean. The fantasy had to end sometime; maybe the ending was what made it shine.

The biggest plane with the biggest cabin I'd ever seen swallowed me and my peaceful heartbreak. I found my seat in the middle section and stared at the speckled carpet like it might wake me from the surreal dream. *Did this really just happen? To me?* I smiled. Six weeks ago I couldn't have scripted this version of me if I tried.

Somewhere on that Hong Kong runway, I started rehearsing how I'd tell the stories. My friends and family. *Oh my God, my friends and family!* I'd been in a six-week coma of presence. Back home felt paused, like someone had hit stop on a cassette. I had no idea what I'd missed. I'd been so full of life and possibility that everyone I loved had slipped to the far edges of the frame.

Already, I missed my Saipan family. I made a mental list of the new friends I'd call first once in L.A., the ones I'd keep. I was deep in denial that the dream was over, but I opened my phone to text Z that I was on my way home. Flight on time customary pleasantries from a long-lost girlfriend.

And right there on my phone screen, there it was. An email from my bosses at The Clinic.

"You're fired."

CHAPTER 18
DICKLESS

"Some endings aren't failures. They're just the universe cutting off your dick supply."

—Someone who gets it

As you can imagine, my flight home was misery on wings.

Thirteen hours of uncontrollable tears drenching a hoodie I wore like armor. Thirteen hours of unspooling all that island-born ease with uncertainty and rewinding straight back into fear of the unknown. Ugly-crying on a plane should be an Olympic event. Center seat, no window to disappear into, chin pinned to my sternum like I could tuck my face back into my own ribs. If it were a sport, I was on mile twenty-six, enduring the whole suck-ass predicament at once. I faked sleeping whenever a flight attendant floated by; one kind eyebrow and we'd have diverted to the nearest runway, and we didn't have one because we were flying over the entire width of the biggest ocean in the world. I was wrecked. It felt like my dad had died all over again. Fuck, this sucks.

For a year I'd built The Clinic, my reputation, my technique, my compassion for men's suffering. I'd learned how to serve, how to care, how to lead. I'd found a voice with men and a calling I'd never seen coming. It mattered. And now it was...gone. Just like that. What the fuck.

Okay, I'd been away longer than anticipated. I am hard to replace, but not impossible. They probably found someone cheaper with more skills. That's just business, right? Sure. But was this fair?

Except I was still answering emails from across the Pacific, still checking in, still carrying the weight of that place like a spare organ. And then they fired me, with a single-line email.

You know those moments when the world tilts so hard you question your sanity? That had been my last year. But getting fired without the courtesy of a conversation felt like the universe upping the ante on betrayal. It dangled adventure like a diamond, then yanked it off my finger.

It hurt. Deep.

In L.A., I dragged myself through customs with swollen eyes, sour breath, and the same carry-on that had housed my whole life for six weeks; four outfits, one pair of flip-flops, one pair of workout shoes and a couple new bathing suits. I stared at that bag in the snaking line and wondered why I'd ever needed more than this floating closet.

At the kiosk, I squared up to the face scanner, puffy, dead behind the eyes, and prayed the machine would glitch. I have never wanted to fail a test so badly. *Please send me back. I can't face whatever waits past those sliding doors.*

No such luck. Customs waved me through into the good ol' U.S. of A. My phone buzzed on the escalator: castmates saying my flight had been the last one out before the storm slammed the island shut. The airport was destroyed. All flights were grounded. It wasn't just any storm, it was a Category 5 super typhoon, the biggest to hit The Mariana Islands in 150 years.

Shit. If that isn't a metaphor for the ruin of my life, I don't know what is.

Guilt hit like backwash from the typhoon. I should've been there with my island family, sandbagging doors, hauling palm fronds, picking glass from the roads. Why did I get airlifted out of one storm only to land in another? Just days ago I'd sipped absurdly expensive tea with the mayor and laughed with my Saipan crew; now everything was splintering, both there and here. The island and I were both absorbing life-altering damage.

Z met me at arrivals. He looked... different. Almost lonely and sad, but threaded with hope, like a man scanning a manifest for a name that proves his person survived. I hugged him, body present, spirit still in Saipan. He cried and said he'd missed me. Being the one left behind is always harder, and I knew that, but I couldn't meet him where he was. I felt hollow. Heartbroken. Halfway on the island.

We barely spoke on the drive. I told him I couldn't process the loss of my job yet. I wasn't ready to turn and look at it. And then there was the email: return your laptop and keys ASAP. As if I'd never existed there. As if I hadn't helped build that place from the first empty calendar to a full roster of broken dicks and redemption arcs.

I'd believed I had equity, both emotional and logistical. Sweat and spreadsheets. I thought I mattered. Maybe that was the sharpest cut: discovering I was replaceable.

Jet-lagged and running on fumes, I walked into The Clinic the next morning. I smiled. I gave away hugs, more from programming than connection. I was cordial, kind, even gracious. They'd already hired a nurse, a credentialed bargain at half my rate. "Nothing personal," the subtext read. "Just business."

I could nod at the logic, but my gut knew better. I'd been in The Clinic before there were even dicks on the calendar. Before intake or consent forms, before protocols, before anyone knew what the hell we were doing. I'd built that place with creative sweat, spreadsheets and soft skills. And now? Poof. Erased.

I didn't fight to stay. I'd just come off a $35 million Chinese TV series. I was a storyteller, not a dick fixer. It had never really been about the dicks for me anyway, it was about what they gave me: identity, worth, power, connection, a strange new safety with men I'd never had before.

Still, I knew the truth I didn't want to say out loud: if they hadn't fired me, I wouldn't have left. I would've kept grinding until my body quit. That job was armor. Anchor. Alibi. Maybe the universe knew I needed to be cut loose. Like when I threw out my back as a waitress, I didn't stop serving until my spine staged an intervention.

So I left. Gracefully. Respectfully. Quietly shattered.

Their decision felt like punishment for wanting a different dream. From their side, all they saw was a deserting soldier: me posting pics in paradise while they were drowning in dicks. To them I was too segmented. Too unavailable. Too...alive.

And just like that, I was out. No job. No income. No purpose. No island to distract me from my demons. No appetite for the life I'd come back to. I moved through my house like a ghost. Even the dogs stared at me like I was a stranger who smelled like ocean and loss.

Reentering my community of friends and family back in the states felt impossible. I tried brunch, hiking and the gym gossip sessions I used to love. But I couldn't relate to anyone anymore. What I'd lived through on that island felt so surreal, so cellular, it made home read like a phony stage set. Food tasted off; too sweet, too engineered. Traffic pressed a palm over my mouth. Conversations skimmed like decaf: warm, flavorless, safe. L.A.

could be fascinating, sure, but nothing pulsed like that island. And I didn't even get to ride the high; the rug yanked out before my feet found it.

After a couple nights of sleeping off jetlag and depression, I told Z everything. The island. The hikes. The lack of control. The strange, holy stillness. How the locals called me "Betty," my character's name, and how it fit like a dress I'd forgotten I owned. How I'd felt like me again or maybe for the first time. I lived awake, electric, inhabited.

I told him how the idea of sex had drifted back like a long-lost friend waving from across a street. People flirted with me. I flirted back. I didn't do anything, but I wanted to—God, I wanted to. That wanting alone felt like an organ rebooting.

I told Z I needed touch. To be wanted. To be claimed. I'd spent a year helping men reclaim their sexual power and somehow remained untouched myself. I needed sex, not just chemistry, but full-on reclamation. And then my mouth beat my caution to the finish line:

"What if we tried an open relationship?"

The phrase tumbled out fast, like I'd borrowed courage from my clients; the unconventional ones who wrote their own love contracts. Maybe this was a radical kindness to both of us. Maybe it was my passport back into my body. Or maybe I just wanted an excuse to shave my butthole with a hand mirror. I don't know. Reinvesting in my appearance felt like a breadcrumb trail back to the part of me I'd lost. Breathing again felt that necessary.

Shockingly, and I mean, stop in your tracks, do a triple take and lean in for certainty after the record scratch kinda shocking, Z said yes, almost too quickly.

"I just want you to be happy," he shrugged. "I'll do whatever it takes."

"Wait... so you'll hook up with other people too?" I blinked hard.

He shrugged again. "Yeah. I guess."

"Like, you'll go on dating apps?"

"I mean... maybe."

Suddenly the new idea blew a hole in the ceiling and flooded the room with air. I didn't know what to do with all that space, but I felt awake, electrified even. Could we really hack this? Get what we could give each other (stability, companionship, co-dog-parenting) then outsource the rest (sex, adventure, novelty) without burning the whole house down? A Venn diagram of us in the middle, with permission to borrow the edges elsewhere?

I sold myself a story: if Z dated other women, maybe he'd find his groove again. Maybe whatever jammed him up with me would unstick with someone new. Another woman might hand him back his confidence like a wallet he'd misplaced. Delusional? Possibly. But for one fragile minute, it felt like we were on the same page, ink wet, but possibilities birthing.

We had a charity event coming up at our CrossFit gym, something I'd planned with Z before I left. Men's health awareness with Move-ember: thirty guys, thirty portraits, thirty stories posted once a day on the gym's social media pages. It would all culminate in a live charity workout to honor my dad on the anniversary of his death. Rubber mats, barbell clang, sweat thick in the air, like church, but with kettlebells.

My mom, sister Danny, and my niece drove in for the event. Even my mother suited up and did the workout. When I told her she couldn't smoke between sets, the classy bitch flipped me off and kept squatting. She loved to participate in anything, but not when it interfered with her smoke break. Aside from golf, "cigs" were one of the few things my parents bonded over.

The charity event wrung me out and filled me back up. Friends lined up to tell me who they'd lost; a mom, a dad, both. Maybe misery loves company, or maybe passing grief around the circle makes it lighter to carry. By the end of the day we'd raised about $3,000. Not a fortune, but enough to say, "We remember. We care. We're trying." Even if we were honoring a man who had a lifelong death wish or at least treated his body like a leased car with unlimited miles.

I gave a speech. My mom, too. We begged the room: take care of yourselves, get tested early, listen to your body. My dad knew something was wrong when he stopped peeing right, but he chalked it up to "getting old." By the time doctors looked, cancer was everywhere. No one should die of prostate cancer—it's too easy to catch early. So we told his story the only way we knew how: as a warning label on love and denial, hoping it scared somebody into staying alive.

And just like that, we'd made it. One full year without my dad. My sisters and I staggered through different stages of grief while my mom clung to the highlight reel, romanticizing the shit out of him.

"He was really sweet to me... at the end," she'd float into unrelated conversations.

Yeah, Mom. Because he was dying. Because the cancer drugs and hormones you helped administer forty-five times a day softened him into someone more bearable. He relied on you to pay attention to no less than seventeen alarms on your phone a day, for meds to prolong his existence and ease his suffering. He wasn't kind to you by choice. He was fully dependent on you to survive. But that final version of him wasn't the man we knew. But go ahead, lie to yourself to sleep at night.

A few weeks after the charity event, Z took me to the ballet to see The Nutcracker. Sweet, right? Well, I hadn't set foot in a dance theater since I was 18, the year a doctor benched me for congenital hip dysplasia, in, not one, but both hips. My acting career launch plan had always been to start as a Fly Girl dancer like JLo on the sketch comedy show In Living Color. I thought hip dysplasia was for inbred Labradors born with shitty hips, but apparently, I had it too. Never mind the trophies on the wall from years of competitive dance in my youth; I'd finessed the limits of my birth defect while my joints were still gummy and forgiving. Once my grown-ass-woman hips set, the prognosis landed hard:

"You weren't born to be a dancer, Kristina. You keep dancing, or doing anything high impact, and you'll be in a wheelchair by thirty-five." The doctor shrugged out with zero fucks.

Really doc? Will I be in a wheelchair? Or will I be standing in high-ass-heels all day fixing broken dicks like yours at thirty-five? You shitty doctor with zero sensitivity to an 18-year-old girl who just left home for the first time to study dance at a prestigious dance college, asshole!

Bitterness remained, but really, and always, grief prevented me from even observing professional dancers because watching other bodies do what mine was told not to, felt like pressing on a bruise. Hard. But, for Z, I went anyway; pain was the rhythm of this year. What was one more twirl into despair? The theater smelled like rosin and velvet. Tutus crackled under the lights. The orchestra tuned, then lifted. I sat pinned to my seat, equal parts awe and ache.

After the show, Z drove us home, behaving off. He was jittery and oddly reverent. He kept pointing out the full moon through the windshield. I glanced up. *Yes, full. Yes, beautiful.* But the island had given me my moment with the moon. Here in L.A., the sky felt crowded with noise and neon and loss.

We got home. The dogs detonated into their usual happy chaos, paws tap-dancing on the hardwood, snouts in my purse, tails thwacking my thighs. Z steered me past them and out onto the backyard deck.

"Look at the moon," he said.

Ugh. I don't want to. Drop it already. I thought.

Before I could brush him off, I turned, and he was holding a ring. An actual fucking engagement ring.

I froze.

I did a double take. I would've done a spit take if I had been drinking. Y*ep, that's a ring. Nope, he wasn't on one knee.* The ring wasn't in a velvet box with a tiny spotlight to announce its entrance. He fished it, bare, from his pocket and held it low, like even he wasn't convinced this was a good idea.

Fuck me.

My heart sank. What the fuck was he doing? What part of "I want an open relationship" indicated that I wanted a ring? I felt betrayed. Sick. The dogs jumped around us, playing as if they were the only ones celebrating.

Then I thought of Betty, the girl I was on the island. She didn't want this. She didn't want him or this life anymore. I'd been sleepwalking because I needed a familiar place to land, but deep down I knew he wasn't a man I could say yes to. I wasn't the girl Z started dating. My heart had been broken, incinerated, resurrected, and let loose this year. I'd been split wide open and hurled off a cliff; I had no idea when I'd hit ground again.

The truth slammed me: I'd been lying to myself. I do believe in marriage. I do believe in love. Marriage felt like the most dangerous, holy gamble, handing someone your heart forever and whispering, please be careful with it.

I wanted to be that brave. I wanted to be that safe. I deserved to be protected, loved, cherished, 'til death actually does the parting. I wanted all of it... just not with Z. He wasn't my guy. He'd invested years, time, money in us, and still my gut knew he wasn't my forever person.

"What are you doing?" I choked out, trembling.

"I missed you so much while you were gone. Life is short. I just didn't want to wait anymore."

Fuck.

"But... but... we said we never wanted this." I reached for the pact we'd made.

He searched my face while the dogs pinballed around our ankles. When he understood I wasn't saying yes, he slid the ring back into his pocket like a shoplifter hiding stolen hope.

He shattered. I shattered. He paced and cried, disbelief wrestling humiliation on his face. I sank to the floor, held up only by my own truth. Shame flooded both of us. I could feel our hearts coming apart in tiny, ruthless clicks. And somewhere, little did I know, he had friends and family waiting for the verdict.

Mother fucker.

His proposal was the actual fucking cherry on top of the shit sundae my life had become. And I still couldn't betray myself; not this new, sharpened version of me. No turning back. Z eventually crumpled to the floor and went silent. I felt terrible for him and sick for myself. The dogs licked our tears and kept dropping squeaky toys between us like tiny referees trying to restart play.

Of course I tried to fix it; that's my reflex. The broken parts of me clocked in for overtime. I wanted to pull the splinter from his heart without yanking out my own truth. Could I do both? Probably not. I apologized. I asked why he'd proposed. We had a deal. He knew who I was from the jump. I wasn't trying to end us; I just didn't want a ring or a wedding. That wasn't me. But it didn't matter how carefully I pled my case; a man's ego rarely walks off the field after that hit.

I became the monster. Not my dad. Not some violent ghost from my past. Me. No longer the victim with a tidy backstory, but the woman causing pain to a man who didn't deserve it. What kind of monster rejects a proposal and then asks to stay together? The kind who's scared. The kind who's grieving a pile of losses and clinging to the one familiar body in the room, even if that body no longer wanted to touch hers.

Why, Z? Why did you have to want more than I could give you? Why? Fuck.

There was no clean exit from this nightmare. We had to sit, stew, and suffer. Nothing with Z had been clean for a long time. No black or white, just murky gray. I'd fallen in and out of love with our life too many times to count. We were human and messy, stuck in the hallway between who we were and who we were becoming. Loving Z enough to stay, not enough to marry him—that was hell. And I'd built it, plank by plank, without meaning to.

We stayed anyway. I didn't say yes. I didn't leave. Maybe I was scared. Maybe I was guilty. Maybe I was just too exhausted to dismantle the scaffolding we'd bolted together; dogs, bills, memories, the emotional rubble we kept sweeping into corners. So we downgraded. Partners to housemates. Two ghosts splitting rent and bougie dog food. Roommates in a haunted house.

I kept imagining what it was like for Z to return the ring. Did he drive to the mall, park under those migraine-bright fluorescents, and stand at a glass counter while a clerk with acrylic nails asked, "Reason for the return?" Did he say, "She said no," and set hope on a velvet tray? The scene crushed what pieces of my heart were left.

We floundered and called it a partnership, but it was really a ceasefire. We cohabited, fed the dogs, answered emails, performed productivity. The truth: I couldn't touch him—not out of anger, out of heartbreak. His, mine, ours. And he couldn't touch me; rejection, betrayal, disappointment calcified on his skin like salt. We passed each other in doorways with the careful choreography of museum guards: close enough to watch, too far to feel.

Too hurt to face the pain we'd caused, so we didn't. We numbed with routine. Morning coffee, dog walks, Sunday housecleaning ritual, intact. Stuck in the familiar. I switched gyms to dodge the public awkwardness from our tight-knit community there. At least we didn't have to perform outside the house.

Meanwhile, my career took flight. Three projects dropped in one year: the Chinese TV show, a short film I'd written, produced and starred in, and a feature film I'd been the lead in. Public me soared. Domestic me withered. I needed light, not levity; people who had survived something and still laughed with their whole bodies. Z's laugh had gone to ground. I couldn't dig it up, not anymore.

Eventually I met someone through work who flipped a breaker inside me. I crossed a line and started seeing him. Open relationship, right? That was the story I handed myself. He was also in an open relationship, which made it feel paperwork-safe, like no one would demand exclusivity or, God forbid, feelings from the other.

Z knew. We didn't talk about the details, but he knew. He set one rule: come home at night no matter the hour. So, I did. But every return felt like climbing back into a grave and pulling the lid over my face. The whole arrangement felt like... cheating; not just on Z, but on the entire life we'd engineered together for over half a decade. I couldn't even look my dogs in the eye. Even they seemed to know.

I worked overtime to convince myself I could do "open." I could be that free, poly person who dipped a toe into strangers' orbits and bodies and felt nothing. I could partition my heart like a hard drive, one folder for need, one for numb. I'd get my physical fix without harming anyone. I had permission, right? *Right?!*

Then Z slid into suicidal thoughts. This time it wasn't the performative spiral I'd survived in other relationships; it was the lights going out in his brain chemistry. He even took an online "Do you have depression?" test—ding, ding, ding. He told me how dark it was getting, and I hated myself for not throwing him a rope, for being the storm in his weather system, for doing to him what had been done to me. I was flying; he was drowning. And I couldn't authentically give him more.

The reality gutted me. And yes, in some slow, quiet way, I became the monster in our story. Not out of malice, out of momentum. I chased bliss while the house sagged under the weight of my absence, the way my father had once outrun his own wreckage. I finally saw how addiction can wear a joy-mask while it chews the beams from the inside.

When the holidays came, I bailed. I couldn't do another family gathering with Z in the room while I performed avoidance like it was a ballet. I went home to see my family alone, to escape, again, just like my dad. I fled the life I couldn't control, baptized my choices in "career building," and called the novelty growth.

Then Z's father died, sudden and brutal, right before COVID snapped the world shut. His mom called: his dad had fallen and was in a coma. Before Z even hung up, I had him on a flight leaving within the hour. He froze; I moved. I zipped a bag, shoved in shirts, chargers, vitamins, handed him shoes, called an Uber. I got him out the door before doubt could take root. I didn't know I was sending him straight into a global lockdown that would strand him there with his grief for months; I only knew I couldn't let him miss the goodbye I never got with my dad.

So with Z gone and the world "sheltered in place", I wrote. I healed. I finally heard my own thoughts again. Quarantine, of all things, for me, was beautiful.

Months later, when Z came back, I knew I couldn't do it anymore. I'd already found a place that could hold me, a summer housesitting gig, and I made my exit. I did it gently and slow, the way you leave someone you still respect, even if the love is gone. I tried to stand in his grief with him the way he'd stood with me in mine, but it wasn't enough; we'd both reset our compasses to different norths, and the map we'd shared no longer fit.

So I ended it, for real this time. It took a couple of months to peel our names off the same bills, box up a life, and stitch separate routines, during a pandemic, no less. Not every ending gets a clean goodbye; some don't offer closure at all.

When we finally unraveled, it wasn't a blowout. It was quiet, like a body going cold. Our communication slid from warm calls and emoji-sloshed texts to subject lines and bullet points. Our love didn't die in a single scene; it bled out, slow and stubborn, a wound neither of us wanted to look at. By the end, all that remained was the heavy silence of two people who couldn't save each other. And I still didn't know I was the one who needed saving.

CHAPTER 19
GOODBYE DICK

"If you love a dick, let it go. The memory might be better anyway."

—Still me

Time to say goodbye.

My grandma, Z, and I pulled up to the one and only hospital in my hometown. Night had already fallen; the lobby clocks blinked 6:30 p.m., exactly when I'd told my dad we'd arrive. Z offered to stay in the car with the dogs. My grandma and I just needed to get inside; the rest would have to sort itself out.

We found my sisters, my mom, my brothers-in-law, and, what I'd later learn, some of my dad's closest friends, gathered in a hush that felt heavy and humid, like grief had its own weather. The staff had bent the rules and let us blow past the visitor limit so everyone could say goodbye. The hallway reeked of antiseptic and the vinyl chairs squeaked every time someone shifted their sorrow.

I rounded the corner into his room, and there he was. My dad's body... in full surrender. A thick plastic tube rammed air into him with a clacking insistence that didn't match the soul I knew. He had never wanted this man-made limbo, hung between life and death by machines. And I had put him here. My stomach dropped. If he was going to be on these damn ventilators so I could say goodbye, the least I could do was change the mood in the space.

"Can we get some music on?" I asked the room.

I scanned the faces. "You know Dad. He doesn't want this sad shit. Where's the Heineken?"

Of course, someone had brought his favorite beer. He'd had one every night of his life, and right now he was still, *technically*, alive. I wasn't about to let his last scene break continuity.

"Everyone, take a sip. Even me."

Yeah, me, sober for 17 years. I took a swig, tiny, but I took it. The taste was metallic and skunky, like aluminum regret. I remembered the nasty taste well: the childhood rite of backwash, Dad tipping the last warm inch of his can toward us like he was knighting us with hops.

People chuckled through their tears at the sight of me; the vegan, the CrossFitter, the personal trainer still drowning in student loans for a health degree, the reformed lecture machine who'd finally climbed off her high horse. The girl who hadn't had a drink since that shitty senior-night in high school sendoff. The one who'd sworn off alcohol because of what it did to our family and the world. I didn't want alcohol, the toxic poison I'd resented my whole life, but this sip was for Dad. On his deathbed, I could meet him where he'd lived: at the lip of a can.

I slid the beer into his hand. Why not? He'd held those cans more than he'd held my mom. They were part of what brought him here; the careless habits, the refusal to feel, the nightly numbing, the trapdoor to his private safe room. A cold ring of condensation printed the sheet; the ventilator whooshed; the life-preserving machines hummed like a bad choir.

We started taking turns to say goodbye. His friends went first, filing past with stories and broken smiles. I waited, then waited some more. I almost intentionally went last because I, like him, was a great avoider of feelings. But there wouldn't be another chance. No reshoots. No do-overs. The line inched forward, and the truth pressed in: there was no escaping this goodbye. Not this time.

Through the ICU room windowpane I watched the rotation: his mother, his brother, his friends, my sisters, my mom. One by one they slipped into the room, sat close, whispered whatever needed to be said. The glass kept their words private, and that felt right. Everyone deserved their minute with this complicated man we all knew in different languages.

In the hallway, Z hurried up to me, hands shaking.

"Um... Gus," he whispered. "Our dog... he ate all the perishable food in the car."

"What?"

"He got out of his doggy seatbelt. He ate the grapes and the mushrooms and..."

The poisonous, toxic grapes.

My epileptic dog had just inhaled a charcuterie of doom on the same night my father was dying. I stared at Z, blank, stunned, and also knew the triage order in my bones.

"What would you like me to do right now?" I asked, looking him straight on.

"I need something to induce vomiting."

"Ask the nurses."

"They won't give it to me."

Of course they wouldn't. Liability. Protocol. The antiseptic-smelling no that hospitals sterilize into everything. I paced that tiny ward, explaining to anyone in scrubs that my dad was dying in the ICU and my dog needed saving now. Heads shook. "Not allowed." I swallowed the explosion building in my throat.

"There's a pharmacy down the street," I told Z. "You'll have to go. Google it. Figure it out. I'm sorry."

He nodded through tears and bolted, unsure and already grieving, knowing he'd have to save Gus alone. He usually leaned on me for the hard calls. Me, our relationship's permanent pack mule for the mental load. Me, the protector. Me, the project manager. Me, with courage on tap. I could act and not feel, but not for both fronts at once. My family needed me. My dad needed me. I needed me. I need my own steadiness, my own hand on my back.

So, I went still, dropped into a surreal calm and watched Z scurry away, uncertain of himself. I don't know why, but I'd always stayed grounded in a crisis. Maybe I had a gift, or a trauma response, or both.

I spun on my heels and headed back to the hallway outside my dad's room. Finally my turn. No one else left—just me and my dying dad.

Fuck. This can't be happening.

I scanned the ICU corridor one last time, half-hoping someone would sneak back in and buy me another minute, half-trying to script what in the actual fuck I was about to say. I'm a writer, an actor, the girl with a quippy line for everything, and my mind was... blank. Shame happily jumped in.

Why didn't I think of anything to say before this moment? I had three and a half years to write an Oscar-worthy speech for my father's dying minutes, and not once did I rehearse it. Of course. I really am just like him, aren't I? Thanks, Dad, for not even preparing me to say goodbye to you, ya' dick.

I pushed into the room, and eased the door shut. The machines owned the air: the ventilator whooshed like a metronome; monitors ticked out their cold little truths. Antiseptic bit my nose. The shitty fluorescents hummed. Plastic tubes rose and fell with every borrowed breath. And only the sweat leaping from my arm pits warmed the air.

I trembled, my breath riding high in my chest. I was still afraid of this man, afraid to be alone with him, even as a shell, unconscious, incapable of hurting me with a look or a line. My nervous system didn't get the memo that it was safe; around him it never had.

I sat beside my dad and took him in. What had happened to this man? Once the king of his community; now a body waiting for permission to go. He looked like a dummy doll propped up by hospital pillows and technology, not the man that I knew.

Courage hijacked my hand and sent it toward his. I*s this the first time I've ever held his hand?* His hand was warm. Not as warm as I'd begged for on the phone, but warm enough. Blood still trickled through. He was still there, even if just barely.

"Hi, Dad," I choked out. My voice did that thing it does when terror grips my throat, dropping to a thin whisper, like sound trying to tiptoe past danger. I'd spent a lifetime afraid of saying the wrong thing, of getting it wrong and paying for it. This moment was no different.

His fingers twitched. Did he hear that?

The nurse had sworn he could still hear and feel us, that even sedated and sinking, the brain keeps a door cracked. I chose to believe her. Faith felt easier than science.

"It's your big girl," I whimpered, the words shrinking me back into the small, braced child I always became around him.

Another ripple under his skin. His eyes stayed shut, but tears slipped from the corners and tracked into his hairline.

Fuck. He can hear me. Now this really matters.

"Dad... I love you. And I'm... I'm so sorry."

The fuck did I just say? Sorry? To him? The sentence left my mouth before my mind caught up.

His body answered: larger spasms, more tears. The more I spoke, the more his face wept.

"I'm sorry for… I am sorry for holding you to such a high standard my whole life."

I listened to myself like I was eavesdropping on a stranger. Something bigger had my mouth by the reins, and I let it pull.

"I only did that because I saw the best in you. I knew what you were capable of, and I wanted that good man. I wanted him all the time. I wanted you to see him, too. I know you did the best you could. I see that now. And I'm sorry I couldn't see it before. I'm sorry it took me this long. You were an amazing dad. And I'm so fucking lucky I got to have you."

I lifted his hand to my cheek. For the first time in my life that lukewarm, calloused, golfer's palm felt… safe.

"I am who I am because of you, for better or worse. I have you in me. Your voice. Your spirit. Your talent. And I promise I won't waste any of it. I promise I'll sing for you. I'll chase every single dream I've ever had for you. I'll do it for both of us. Everything you didn't get to do. Okay?"

His body shuddered like a chord struck too hard. Tears kept coming.

"You gave me that courage, Dad. That confidence to follow my heart. You did. Because I knew you loved me. I didn't need to hear it. I always knew. I will always be the little girl on your shoulders looking at the moon, building our dreams together."

My own tears soaked his cracked knuckles. And then the truth landed, clean and undeniable: I had given my dad the apology I'd spent years waiting to receive from him. I hadn't planned it. I hadn't even wanted to say it. But the apology arrived, and I let it. In that exchange, I unlatched his cage and mine. We were both, finally, free to rest in peace.

The whole thing felt like an out-of-body experience. The girl who walked in shaking, small, braced, wordless, got shouldered aside by a steadier version of me: older, clearer, stitched up in places I didn't know were torn. She handled the moment like she'd trained for it. One shot only. Said what we both needed to hear. Didn't flinch.

Before I let go of him, I laced my fingers through his and studied them like artifacts. Those ridiculous olive tricks flashed back. The way he'd place ten little black olive helmets on ten Denton fingers, pop-pop-pop into a laughing mouth. Quirky, showy, and pure Bob. I giggled, yep, *I inherited that exact brand of improv nonsense*, pressing his knuckles to my cheek.

Fucking asshole. Where did that guy go?

Then I kissed his hand and looked him square in his closed, wet eyes, "I love you, Dad. Goodbye, for now."

We gathered again, my sisters, my mom, me by his side and offered up "From This Moment" by Shania Twain like a lopsided prayer. We were painfully off-key, sniffling between lines, but we sang the whole damn thing. I could hear him in my head, grinning: "Who cares! Let it out! It feels good!" He always wanted volume and freedom of expression, not perfection.

After we wrapped the song, the nurses slipped in and asked us to wait in the hall while they pulled the tubes out. Right, messy, unsexy housekeeping. Probably for the best that we didn't learn exactly what comes up with a ventilator; some mysteries can stay medical.

So we filed out. Thirty of us—family, friends, ghosts-in-training—flattened against the corridor like a quiet crime scene. Overhead lights flickered. Shoes squeaked and then didn't. No one cracked a joke. No one filled the air. We'd poured every ounce of ourselves into that room, and now all we could do was lean back into the hallway wall and surrender, to divine timing, to whatever mercy lets a stubborn body finally let go.

While we waited, Z slipped back into the hallway looking shaken, pharmacy bag crumpled in his fist. He'd managed to induce vomiting in Gus, but we'd need an emergency vet now. Except our small-ass town rolled up the sidewalks at 6 p.m.; the nearest after-hours clinic was an hour away. Of course it was. I squeezed his arm. "We'll handle it after. Together. Right now, I have to say goodbye to my dad." My brain had room for exactly one emergency.

We filed back into my dad's room and took our stations around the bed like a ragged choir. I scanned faces: quiet sobs, open-mouthed grief, flat stares, soldier-still jaws. Shock sat on some shoulders like a lead cape. Had anyone here watched a person die before? Maybe none of us had. Whatever our credentials, this was first-time territory: my father, our only subject, and the only lesson we'd ever get.

No one teaches the etiquette of this vigil: sitting still while a body winds down. Just monitors, breath, and the thud of inevitability. The nurses had said it was over; there was nothing left to push against.

Is this why people bring in priests? To fill the void between life and death?

We didn't have a priest, and I'm certain my dad wouldn't have wanted one. Not with his trauma history. So, we did the hardest thing... nothing. We let death come when it was ready for him.

"It could be twenty minutes, maybe an hour," the nurse had warned. "His heart's strong. It may take time."

I edged up by his face, pressed my forehead to his temple, and stroked that beautiful hair; still full, still stubborn, a trophy he'd grown long through both chemo and radiation treatment like a quiet middle finger to cancer.

Resting on his temple might have been the closest I'd ever been to him. Something in me opened, or dropped in, and a melody rose without asking. I didn't recognize it. I didn't need to. I just hummed, low and steady, like a hand on a back guiding a soul toward its final exit.

Then the door clicked and his best friend, Paul (fucking, Paul) finally made it, commuter traffic be damned, seventy-five miles behind him. I looked up, then turned my mouth to my dad's ear.

"Paul's here, Dad. He made it. Paul's here."

"I'm here, Bobby" Paul squeaked out and grabbed his arm.

Three seconds later, my dad took his final breath. And died. At 8:08 p.m. on a Tuesday.

And there it is. The time of death spells BOB on the clock, doesn't it? Fucking fitting. The asshole wasn't gonna go out without a bang and a wink. Always making a lasting impression.

The flatline you hear in movies isn't melodrama; it's accurate. Death is a single, unforgiving tone. I closed my eyes. My right hand rested on the top of his head, forehead still pressed to his temple and then a force rushed through my hand, a clean shove of wind under skin. My eyes snapped open. I knew, without logic, without language, that my dad's soul had just slipped past my palm on its way out. O*h, fuck.*

Now, I didn't believe any of that woo-woo shit. I'd never heard of anyone feeling a soul exit a body outside of corny films. But there, in that antiseptic stench of death, I knew what it was. God, the universe, my dad—whatever the fuck was working the strings—yanked me like a marionette and handed me a moment I couldn't deny. The feeling tilted my axis, a spiritual recalibration I didn't ask for, a quick flash of the divine telling me to pay attention.

I didn't have the capacity, or the time, to unpack the esoteric bullshit of it all. The show had to move on. I had to go save my dog, Gus. I couldn't lose him, too. Not on the same night.

I stood and asked the nurse for scissors. No plan, just instinct. While everyone else took their last looks, I snipped a lock of my dad's hair and slid it into a little bag for my mom. A strange, sacred craft project. I caught the confusion on my family's faces and didn't care. I needed something of him that would last.

I gave my dad one last look, and braced for the next mission. *Goodbye, forever, Dad. Not the performative kind you toss over your shoulder to be dramatic. The real forever. This is it. I will never see you again. Not ever. From here on out you're a story and a Ziploc of hair. Goodbye, Dad. Fuck. What the fuck?*

I pivoted on wobbly heels and walked out. That was it. The space between my dad and me, the gap I'd spent years trying to close, sealed itself and then blew wide open, once again, expanding into the infinite darkness. Time ran out on any new line of dialogue, any new glance, any new... anything. Our story, over. Full stop. The end.

Now, I had to save my dog.

CHAPTER 20
DICK PARTY

"All any dick really wants is to be celebrated."

—My last lesson

Within an hour of my dad's death, my mom's phone rang; an unknown number with that brisk, businesslike voice: the organ donation team. My dad had always carried the little sticker on his license, so of course they called. You have to admire the courage, or the clinical dissociation, it takes to do that job. They can't pause for our grief; if they're going to save anything, they have to move now.

The timing didn't shock me. What did? That there was anything left worth taking. I'd assumed cancer had taken a shit on every cell in my dad's body. Turns out, it hadn't. The saintly organ pirates found something not only usable but urgently needed: my dad's eyes. *What the fuck, universe?* My dad's soulful eyes, my favorite of his features, the part of him that always told the truth even when his mouth couldn't. Those eyes, those soft, sparkling proofs that he loved me, would go on seeing after he stopped.

Poetic. Tragic. A cosmic prank. A bittersweet ending to his life and our relationship. The best part of him lived on, and I'd never see it. I didn't know whether to laugh or rage. Angry at the timing, grateful that someone else might catch a beam of the love those eyes gave me.

Z and I slid into the car and gunned it toward the emergency vet to save Gus. The drive stretched forever. Streetlights smeared into comets; the highway narrowed to windshield and white lines. I went quiet and hollow, like I'd stepped into the eye of a storm—strangely calm, uneventful, one thin breath before the next wall of weather hit.

Inside the vet clinic, the aromatic blend of dog piss and dander crash landed on my tongue. The vets were kind, efficient. "It'll be a thousand dollars for detox," one said, already prepping the chart. A thousand dollars we didn't have. Z was unemployed, and I was a glorified front-desk girl at The Clinic still. He never traveled with credit cards, of course he didn't, so we called our roommate, sent him digging through drawers for anything plastic with a pulse.

We scraped together $500 of usable credit. The vet needed the rest up front. So we dialed CareCredit, sat on hold while cheerful saxophones mocked us, and begged a stranger to loan us the other half. My dad's body was getting colder by the minute while I recited my Social, my address, my income, hoping my past choices made me worthy of $500 more to save my fucking dog. After an hour of scrambling, we got the ding of approval. The vets whisked Gus to the back to pump charcoal through his belly and babysit his kidneys.

We left him there overnight, signed the paperwork with shaky hands, and drove back through the dark to my sister's house, one dog in the backseat and not much hope in the front. Every time my phone lit up, I braced for the call that Gus hadn't made it.

He did. Thank God. A thousand dollars and a black slurry later, Gus pulled through. With the dog stabilized, I pivoted back to the family triage. The next week blurred, casseroles on the porch, lasagnas with handwritten notes, neighbors ringing the bell and folding us into quick, awkward hugs. Between drop-ins and paper plates, we planned my dad's celebration of life. He'd always said funerals were shitty and sad. He wanted a party: drinks poured high, karaoke cranked louder, stories told, and plenty of shit talked about him—his exact request. On brand, Bob. On brand.

I flipped into go-mode, the only setting my parents ever modeled: do, don't feel. So I gave myself a job; design the celebration-of-life pamphlet. I spent hours hunting for the photo that would become Bob Denton's last impression on his friends and family forever. High-stakes, high-pressure curation of a whole human. I tried to crawl inside his head and pick what he'd pick... and then I snorted, because I didn't actually know what this man liked. Not really. We'd never sat shoulder-to-shoulder and ranked his angles.

Losing a parent feels like losing a leg; you can still move, but you'll be hobbling the rest of your life. The foundation buckles. Everything you've ever known shifts a few inches to the left. You become a fraction of yourself. Overnight, the world looked tinted and murky, like I was wearing dirty contacts I couldn't swap out. New normal: permanently smudged. New color palette: bleak.

But the party? Epic. My sisters and I made sure of it. We booked the golf clubhouse (abso-fucking-lutely we did), dressed the tables in tacky golf crap and stacked his favorite trophies like centerpieces. We printed "Fun Facts About Bob" cards—deep cuts only the real fans would know. We went all in; call it our last shameless bid for his approval.

People poured in from every pocket of his life; coworkers, golf buddies, family we hadn't seen since the Clinton administration. Three hundred, give or take, all of them his audience. They told stories and talked glorious shit, exactly as requested. Karaoke cranked. Drinks flowed. Classic Bob.

My sister, Lucy, grabbed the mic.

"Everyone loved my dad in their own way, but one thing we thought to ourselves for sure was...God, you're a dick."

The crowd roared. Everyone knew she was right. And then over the honest laughter, one of his other best friends shouted:

"But he was *our* dick!"

Lucy went on to share a story I had never heard.

"My dad called me one day after his first round of chemo was over and his latest test results showed he was, surprisingly, improving...

"'Lucy, I'm gettin' better,' he chirped.

"'Oh, yeah?'

"'You know what? I figured it out.'

"'What's that, Bobber?' (she called him that)

"'It's because I pickled myself.'"

The crowd chuckled, confused. Lucy continued.

"I said, 'You did what, Dad?'

"'I pickled myself with Heineken and Marbs. The cancer has nothing to feed on.'"

"Fuckin' Bob," Lucy sighed, and everyone laughed their asses off, knowing exactly how on brand it was for him to convince himself with that logic.

Yeah, dad, the careless lifestyle that got you here is definitely going to save your life. I thought.

When it was my turn to speak, the oldest-daughter pressure sat squarely on my sternum. I felt like I had to represent my mom and, somehow, him. Make him proud. Land the plane with something people would carry out into the parking lot and remember.

First, I queued up a gift: one of his friend's sons—an actual singer—doing "More Than Words" by Extreme. Dad loved that song. Of course he did; he couldn't always say what he felt. His eyes did it for him, those eternal eyes now living in someone else's body. The kid nailed it. People cried, probably because they knew the same version of my father I did, the man bigger than words, beyond tidy description.

Then I took the mic. I had no speech, just impulse. So I did the only appropriate, wildly inappropriate thing: I told the story of how my sisters and I found my parents' porn.

Not Blockbuster porn. Their porn. The 1992 homemade sex tape. Fuck yeah.

My mom covered her face. "You are not going to do this."

"Oh, I absolutely am."

I am Bob's daughter. I wasn't about to let my last public word about this complicated man be beige. Not the man I spent my life trying to understand. This was my moment to tell the truth the way our family always did – too loud, a little wrong, and somehow exactly right.

I started with one Thanksgiving in 2008, right after my parents moved out of our childhood home and into a fresh, echoey house that still smelled like cardboard and Windex. My sisters and I were all in our twenties, boomerang kids who'd ping-ponged in and out between college flameouts and relationship resets. Boxes were stacked everywhere like a maze, and one of them, parked conveniently beside the seventy-inch flat screen, was a time capsule: VHS bricks and mini-DVs from the 80s and 90s. In those home movies, Dad was the auteur with the camcorder, and my aunt the on-screen narrator who announced the date and holiday while we feral children screamed through the background.

Since the entire family had miraculously gathered in one room, I decided we were doing Home Movie Night. I planted myself on the carpet inches from the TV, fished out the mini-DV camcorder (bless the drawer goblins for not losing it), plugged in the cables, and dragged the box into my lap.

My sisters and their half-drunk boyfriends sank into the couch. Mom clattered around the kitchen cleaning (per usual, with zero help, also per usual). Dad had already gone to bed, which was odd, he usually outlasted us on holidays.

We howled at footage of our wobbling first steps, Mom's belly with the twins, and tried to resurrect ancient competition routines that once felt like the Olympics. Somewhere between "remember that leotard?" and "oh my God, those bangs," I heard Mom call out, very casually,

"Maybe... don't watch too many of the blank ones."

Clocked. Noted. Immediately ignored.

Because chaos was my love language, I plucked a mini-DV with no label and slid it in. I hit play.

The screen flashed white. I leaned back to get the full picture.

There. It. Was.

A woman's ass, bent over, both holy exits cleared for takeoff. I blinked.

Then, a dude's hand entered the frame and, uh, politely greeted a portal. My brain stalled.

Then, as if dispatched by Central Casting, a very confident, very upright dick made its entrance, headed for one of the aforementioned doors.

Hard cut to silence on the couch.

The moment I heard the soft rock music on the tape; music that doubled as a "do not enter" sign to my parents' bedroom all through the 90's, I knew exactly what this was: My fucking parents. My parents fucking. That was my mom's asshole and vagina. And that was my dad's dick. His DICK. Of all the dicks a woman will see in her life, this is NOT the one you want to see. Not now. Not ever.

Did I mention my parents owned a 70-inch TV screen? And that my sisters, their boyfriends, and my five-year-old niece were all present? Also, my mother, still in the kitchen, while a feature presentation of her most private geography played in IMAX.

Seconds into this midnight special, I deployed the only life-saving measure I had: I hurled the camcorder across the room.

Cords snapped and whipped. Everyone screamed. My mom covered her face and sprinted to her bedroom like the house was on fire. My twin sisters shot off the couch in opposite directions, circled, and collided mid-living room like drunk figure skaters. Our bodies folded—laughter, terror, horror, disgust—hitting all the notes at once.

Then I remembered my niece. She's five. *Oh, God, no.*

I crouched to her level. "Hey, baby girl... what did you see?"

"I saw Nana's butt," she said, delighted, the way kids announce finding a lucky penny.

Oh shit. This is real. We are gonna be scarred for life. There's no going back from this.

It was painfully on brand for my family: nothing ever "normal" or "classy" without slapstick chaos crashing the scene.

It took hours for the house to unclench. Mom never came out, bedroom door shut, lights off, shame on a feedback loop. If it were up to her, she'd still be in there, rearranging the blinds and her regret.

My sisters and I crafted our parents' porn names. We couldn't remember exactly how they went. Was it your pet's first name and your middle name? Or the street you grew up on and your middle name? We couldn't figure it out. We landed on Lizzie Plumber and Ray Castle, strong, solid, and porn-y.

By Thanksgiving morning, Dad was up, which meant he'd already been briefed on our midnight IMAX of parental nudity. Normally the man didn't blush; he was shameless and owned every bit of his chaos. Until this very fine holiday.

I sashayed over to him before dinner, gravy boats sailing by, football murmuring in the background. I locked eyes with him. "So, Dad..."

He cut me off, eyes darting away. "Don't even think about it."

"No, no. Listen." I held my hands up. "Of course it's funny, but it also sucks. That was private, and some genius decided to dump every tape into one box during the move. How dare they. I'm not here to roast you. I won't even tease you about your porn name, promise. I just wanted to say... congrats. I'm proud of you. Proud you two were still... you know... gettin' it in after we were born. That's hopeful. It makes me happy for you. And honestly, my takeaway-"

He went very still, jaw set like he was bracing for a punch.

"I gotta say... I'm impressed."

"Huh?" He blinked, as if waiting for the trapdoor.

"Now I know if I have a son, he's going to have some great genes."

That's right, I complimented my dad's dick right to his face.

What are you gonna do now, Bob?

I could think of nothing more horrendous to say to him and felt like I deserved to have my moment. If I was going to be subjected to seeing his dick, which I didn't ask for, then he was going to hear some heinous shit from his first born in return. Was it really a great, dick? I have no idea. I didn't actually look long enough to evaluate it, but I needed something, anything to make his discomfort all the more painful. And it worked.

My dad flushed scarlet, and for the first time in his life he had nothing. Not a quip, not a dodge, not even a grunt. Just a frozen, red scowl. I'd embarrassed him. Ha. Point, me. I'd finally beaten him at his own sport, razor wit, dark-ass humor, and the audacity to say the one thing no sane person would. There was no comeback left in his arsenal.

I am the reigning monarch of this family's comedy throne, both king and queen. Thank you very much. Eat shit, Dad. I learned from the best. You only have yourself to blame.

God, telling that story felt delicious. The memorial crowd didn't know whether to cackle or dry heave, so they did both, while my mother covered her face and hunted the nearest exit for a mercy cigarette. But they weren't thinking about my dad being dead, were they? *You're welcome, everyone.* I handed them unapologetic, fucked-up laughter as anesthesia. That's exactly what he would've wanted: for the room to know his daughter thought he had a tremendous dick. *You're welcome, Dad.*

We closed the night exactly his way; karaoke mic in one hand, drink in the other. Well, everyone else drank; I just sang. People got gloriously shitfaced in pure Bobber fashion. Fine by me, drunk ears are very forgiving.

My sisters and I stood shoulder-to-shoulder, shaky but grinning, singing the songs he loved. The songs he raised us on. His friends drifted up beside us. The room thrummed with stories and cheap speakers and memory. I could feel him in the corner, smirking, tossing out a sarcastic aside, daring us to go for the high note.

Then a song I barely knew glued itself to my ribs: "Space Oddity." Bowie's voice floated; haunted, hypnotic, a little lonely. It was my father. A man always just out of reach, orbiting on the edge of our atmosphere. Never fully grounded. Never fully ours.

"And I think my spaceship knows which way to go..."

He was the astronaut of our family—solitary, mysterious, adrift—brilliant in his own busted way. A man who needed a mic, a nine-iron, and a buzz to plug into people, yet somehow, he still left stardust everywhere he went. That night, that song became his anthem.

And just like that... he was gone. Back to the stars.

EPILOGUE
LIFE AFTER DICKS

"No dicks were harmed in the making of my freedom... at least not intentionally."

—Everything I know

I found a note under my windshield once. In the dark, after one of my baby sisters' weddings, the reception glitter still stuck to my scalp, heels hooked in my fingers, the parking lot humming with crickets and late-night idling. A white corner peeked out from under my windshield wiper like a parking ticket from the universe. My stomach dropped. I lifted the blade; dew slicked my knuckles. Not a ticket. A note. The highway to L.A. yawned south, and there I was, twenty-something and unlaunched, standing between a backseat full of centerpieces and a future I couldn't see, holding a piece of paper like it might tell me where to go.

His handwriting hit me before the words did: that perfect, unmistakable grocery-store block print. All caps. Lines straight as aisles. Sharpie pressed just hard enough to seep through the back. Neat. Uniform. Zero wobble. It was the same script he used to price peaches and announce WEEKLY SPECIALS, as if letters themselves had to behave. The penmanship said he cared, at least about how things looked, and for a second it felt like a hand on my shoulder in the bright light of a produce section.

"KIKS, EACH OF YOUR SISTERS LOVES, ADMIRES, AND RESPECTS YOU. NO ONE ELSE IS LIKE YOU. I GOT LUCKY YOUR MOM RESCUED ME. GOT LUCKY AGAIN, I GOT RESCUED BY YOU. IN YOUR SMALL TIME, YOU SAW THE WONDERS OF THE WORLD. AND WITH YOU ON MY SHOULDERS, I SAW THEM, TOO."

My dad never called after I left for college at eighteen. Not a "how's school?" Not a "still breathing?" No text. No check-ins. Nothing. But this quiet billboard of a note under my wiper landed harder than any hug.

I didn't know what to do with his words. Praise from my dad always arrived sideways for me; rare, confusing, slightly slurred, never face-to-face. So I cycled through the usual: pissed, then annoyed, then heartbroken, then confused. My default setting with him.

What did he mean by this? What did he ever mean with his confusing backhanded compliments formed with beer logic?

Still, I folded the paper and slid it into my wallet. Over the years I kept pulling it out, re-reading it like a sacred text, sniffing it for subtext, for loopholes, for the receipt of love I could finally cash. Only recently did it click – that was his "I love you." That was him saying I'd saved him. That the life he might've had without my mom, or without me clinging to his neck, pointing at the moon, would've been worse than the messy one we got.

I'd spent years waiting for my dad to show up, to honor me, to protect me. What I didn't see until he was gone was that I'd been protecting him. Protecting both of us from the truth that he never got what he needed from his parents. No one taught him how to show up, stay soft, or be still. You can't give what you never got, unless you learn how, painfully and late.

He didn't know softness without a guard; emotion needed a punchline; presence required a cigarette and a Heineken. In his last year, and mine after he died, I started clocking the odd, off-brand ways he loved: karaoke as communion, one-liners timed like cymbal crashes, turning nobodies into fucking celebrities for showing up to his tee time or sliding onto a clubhouse barstool. He sprinted from anything he couldn't fix, our family, my mom, himself, and chased pleasure like oxygen: golf, beer, Whitney, Sinatra, laughter, applause. They weren't just exits; they were offerings. He gave what he had, like mentoring a kid into a college golf scholarship, preaching Beyoncé from a golf cart like Scripture. Maybe that was his love language all along.

My dad was the sun. He could warm you and scorch you in the same breath. His light could make things grow, and it could fry the earth. I spent my life learning to orbit him without burning, trying to earn his attention without getting singed. I wanted him to choose me, to see the real me. Not the girl who performed well, but the little kid on his shoulders pointing at the moon, saying her first word; the woman at his bedside, humming love into his ear as he died.

And when the moment came, really came, it was me who made the call to keep him alive just long enough for that goodbye. Some part of me still needed his warmth. One last hit. One last beam of light before he was gone.

In the end I realized my dad *did* want to live, just not the way I thought he should. He didn't live for longevity; he lived loud. For the moment. He wasn't trying to preserve his body; he was trying to use it. Burn through it. Squeeze out every drop of joy. He wasn't careful or preventative. But he was present, at least when it mattered to him.

Maybe that's why the Hunter S. Thompson quote I slipped into his celebration pamphlet always felt like his North Star. Maybe he understood it long before I did:

"Life is not a journey to the grave with the intention of arriving safely in a well-preserved body, but rather to skid in sideways, thoroughly used up, totally worn out, and loudly proclaiming, 'Wow, what a ride!'"

And holy shit, what a ride it was.

A few months after lockdown lifted, my house-sitting gig ended, and I officially moved out of the home I'd been living in for nearly six years with Z. He stayed in the house with the dogs. It felt easier for them. Gus relied on stability for his seizures. "We'll figure out joint custody when I'm ready," Z said, like it was a cable-installation window: sometime between never and hell freezing over.

I spent the next few months trying to find a permanent place on my own that I could afford without employment, during a pandemic. *Yeah, good luck.* I bounced in and out of other housesitting gigs, sometimes on friend's couches, sometimes overnight in my car. Once I found a place of my own, Z kept punting. Then, without warning, he moved to Mexico to be with his family and took the dogs with him. No meetup. No handoff. No goodbye. Just gone, like I'd never existed. I dropped to the tile in my new studio in a nervous-breakdown heap like someone had ripped my children out of my arms and I was powerless to stop it.

Part of me believed I deserved it; for leaving, for asking for more, for detonating the life we'd built. Part of me felt like collateral damage to a man's wounded ego; like my pain didn't count because his was louder. And in some ways, it was. I left; he stayed in the silence, in the shame of what didn't work. Just like Saipan, I chased a horizon, and he held the shore.

Then, while Z was in Mexico, one of my dogs died. Gus, the epileptic, the one I'd always feared wouldn't make it without me. I'd carried that fear in my chest like a razor blade. When it finally sliced through the skin, I wasn't there. No goodbye. Just abandoned hearts, for them and me. That loss broke me more than anything else—more than my dad dying, more than the verbal shrapnel, more than the homelessness, the financial freefall, the collapse of who I thought I was. Losing my dogs was the cost of my freedom, and it nearly destroyed me.

I fell into the deepest shame spiral of my life after that. This one I couldn't pin on my father, or soften with a joke, or outsource to a therapist with a copay. It was mine—fully mine—and it almost swallowed me before I could turn and face it. It forced me to look at the parts I'd outrun: the grief, the shame, the twitchy fear that I was fundamentally unlovable. From there, I had no choice but to begin again.

On the far side of losing my dad, The Clinic, Z, my dogs, and, briefly, my sanity, the lessons kept arriving. Hurt people hurt people. Healing doesn't let anyone off the hook; it loosens the fantasy that they should have known better before they did. Z wasn't trying to destroy me. Maybe, in flashes, he wanted to. Mostly, he was drowning in his pain. Just like my dad. Neither had the tools to stay soft inside their suffering, to stand still in the wreckage of their shame. That didn't make them monsters. It made them human; complicated, unequipped, taught by the world that vulnerability is weakness when it's actually the only way through.

The year after my dad died, The Clinic turned into the wildest stretch of my life. It didn't just school me on men and their dicks; it made me forgive the one I swore I never could. I learned to look past bravado and see ache, to spot shame crouching under silence, to understand that most men aren't dodging love, they're avoiding being seen and found lacking.

It's easy to demonize the people who broke us. It's harder to clock the pain beneath their choices. But that's what the work demanded from me, again and again: tearful, whispered confessions; intake forms scrawled with "I haven't had sex in five years"; flinches that came not from treatment, but from admitting the truth out loud. Holding witness to that cracked me open. If I could cradle their shame without flinching, maybe I could finally turn and face my own.

Lucy told me she went with my dad for a second opinion at UC Davis after he was first diagnosed. The doctor scanned his chart and, almost as an afterthought, said prostate cancer often meant permanent erectile dysfunction. *Your erections will stop. They won't return.* Lucy told me she watched something leave our dad's face. His whole energy field shrank like a kid who'd just been told his puppy died. She thinks that's when he died the first time.

Imagining the news land on my father, through my sister's eyes, crushed me. There it was. My dad, the invincible Bob Denton, had ED His story showed me what men brought to my table before they ever undressed: grief, shame, and the terror that without a working dick, they would disappear forever.

I was never in the room when my clients heard that heartbreaking sentence relayed to them. I only met the aftermath, the solution focused man, the one who didn't want to give up yet.

I'm certain my dad was devastated to know cancer killed his dick, but not enough to change the habits that broke it in the first place. That contradiction, that heartbreak, was what I saw in so many men: the longing to hold onto their power while outrunning the pain that robs them of it.

I didn't go looking for that education or healing. I didn't sign up for a spiritual retreat, or a daddy-issues deep-dive expedition I didn't know I needed. I took a job to pay bills and collect a few unhinged dinner-party stories. But in holding space for their bodies, their confessions, their heartbreak, I softened. I started grieving not just the man my father was, but the boy he never got to be—the man who learned to feel through volume and volatility instead of safety and tenderness.

Every broken dick arrived with a backstory, and so many of those stories rhymed with my father's. Angry men. Ashamed men. Men who didn't know how to love without control, a punch line, or silence. In their detachment, I saw his. In their urgency to be "fixed" without explaining how they'd shattered, I saw his cracks, too.

The Clinic peeled me open slowly, session by session, story by story, dick by dick. It stripped off my armor. It taught me men aren't the enemy, and I'm not broken for wanting their approval or love. I just hadn't learned a clean way to receive love and neither had many of them. Somewhere between penis-pump pratfalls and emotional collapses, between lubed-up latex gloves and accidental therapy sessions, I found something that looked a lot like peace.

This wasn't just a weird chapter; it was a mirror. A dick mirror, if you will (and you must, because I am absolutely gunning for a "dick" world record here). That mirror threw my own hurts, judgments, and unmet needs right back at me, while reflecting to the men on my table that it was okay to be scared. That they didn't have to carry it alone. That we're all wild little humans doing our best with the dull tools we were handed.

I'm not a doctor, nurse, therapist, or any kind of licensed healer. Well, technically, I am still a certified dick fixer. Proudly. Thank you very much. But I'm not here to dispense medical advice. I'm also not here to claim all men are safe. Some aren't. I've met them. I've survived them. But you don't need letters after your name to recognize a man wrestling his demons. I've felt that fight up close, in the tremor of a hand gripping the edge of the table, in the swallow they can't quite get down, in the shame that clings like a second skin. Most of them never got the love they needed and still don't know how to ask for it. So when the ones who found me finally felt safe enough to tell the truth, I believed them.

If anything, the job taught me that men keep measuring masculinity by (dick) hardness, when the measure should be wholeness, or how deeply they can risk vulnerability, be held, and face fear in a world that demands they stay fearless. And I do think the world is tilting, ready for them to soften, to stop armoring over suffering. With the right support, I know they can.

I'd spot former clients "in the wild" sometimes, which was wild in itself. And my first instinct? Run. Not because I was embarrassed, but because I didn't want to embarrass them. I'd never wanted to become a walking reminder of a limp dick. I felt absurdly protective, like I was guarding a state secret, and my mere face might have breached it.

Not long after I left The Clinic, I went to a friend's Christmas party. Twinkle lights everywhere. Ugly sweaters. The "worst tacky ornament" game I invented with my friend years prior. I was debating a fourth sugar cookie when the front door creaked open... and in walked one of my former clients.

Fuck! Adrenaline detonated in my veins. My fight-or-flight chose "fling yourself into idiocy," so I swan-dove behind the refrigerator like it was a fallout shelter. Jesus, take the wheel. Or the crisper drawer.

The hostess, my friend, caught me crouched on her trendy linoleum, scrubbing an imaginary stain like I worked there.

"What the hell you doing, babe?"

"My client is here."

She knew about the job. She knew the stakes. She peeked around the corner and gasped.

"Oh my God. Ron? My neighbor?!"

She cackled, and like any good friend, immediately summoned witnesses to my humiliation.

"This is epic. Highlight of the night!" she announced as a semi-circle formed to watch me unravel.

"Shh! He's going to see me!" I hissed.

More heads popped in. Was I trapped in a mid-budget rom com? No, I was a fully grown woman hiding behind kitchen appliances from an elderly gay man in a festive turtleneck. For his protection. I would've scaled a balcony if there'd been one within lunging distance.

Ron wasn't an ex. Ron wasn't a one-night stand. Ron was a man whose dick I had clinically shocked for six sessions in a dim room while making small talk about retirement accounts and his lover. I wasn't afraid he'd hit on me; I was afraid he'd feel exposed. I didn't want to be the face that reminded him of the time he cried while I gently tugged his testicles out of the vacuum tube.

"He cannot see me," I whimpered.

"Why not?" the peanut gallery asked, fully invested now.

"Because... what if he recognizes me and gets embarrassed? What if he remembers what I know? What if I become a walking, talking shame trigger? What if he sees me and thinks I told all of you he has ED—because he does?!"

They smirked, amused by my need to shrink for a stranger. My friend blinked, soft and direct. "Yeah, but that's not your fault, babe. It's just a ridiculous coincidence. You do realize you deserve to exist, right?"

Damn. She's got me there.

Yes. Technically, I deserved to be there, eating cookies, losing at tacky ornament bingo, existing. But I felt like my presence needed a trigger warning. I wasn't ready to carry shame that wasn't mine anymore, and yet my body still defaulted to shrink-wrap mode: be smaller, be softer, don't be the reason anyone feels anything bad. There's a special kind of exhaustion that comes from apologizing for taking up oxygen. The daddy issues still had me by the ankle, dragging me back in the strangest ways.

And of course, that's when Ron wandered into the kitchen.

Come on, Ron! Fucking hell!

I turned to face the wall like I'd been put in kindergarten time-out. My friend's free hallway therapy hadn't sunk in yet. I even wished, briefly and desperately, for a convenient make-out partner (gender optional) to stage a distraction so Ron would flee the scene out of sheer social mercy.

He walked right past me, plucked a deviled egg from the counter display, and kept moving. Completely oblivious. He never clocked me. Not then. Not ever. I exhaled a whole rosary of thank-yous. I could unpack the Olympic-level absurdity of my response later, in therapy, with diagrams. For now, I was in the clear.

Plot twist: a few months later I moved into that very house and became his neighbor. Like the universe wanted me to Airbnb my shame and extend the stay indefinitely. We ran into each other dozens of times after that and not once did he blink with recognition. I went from clinical dick technician to friendly neighborhood girl. Maybe without the mask, the lubed-up gloves, or the medical zapper in my hand, I was hard to identify.

Honestly, thank God. A deeply disturbed part of me still wanted to shout, "Hey, Ron! Remember me? I'm the reason your blood flow cooperated for Palm Springs!" But I didn't. I let him keep his peace. That's what I was doing in those rooms all along—offering men a chance to reclaim their dignity. And sometimes that meant hiding behind a fridge in a terrible holiday sweater to protect it... and, apparently, mine.

Full circle achieved: from Santa Dick in Tucson to actual Santa Ron at a Christmas party in Silverlake. I'd come a long way.

And so have you. If you've made it this far, thank you. It's been a riDICKculous ride. So I'll leave you with this:

If you're a male-identifying reader, I hope you know you don't have to be hard to be strong. Vulnerability isn't weakness; it's human. The thing you're convinced is broken might be the exact part of you begging to be seen, heard, claimed, and healed.

If you're a female-identifying reader, I hope you stop waiting for men to magically "get it" and get curious instead. Let yourself be surprised by the guys you wrote off. See the pain hiding behind the peacocking. Remember: softness isn't submission, it's strength. We are wired to lead the inner world, so let's champion that gift and help the ones who are struggling, without setting ourselves on fire to keep anyone warm.

If you're somewhere in between or gloriously outside the binary, I hope you feel seen, too. This story isn't just mine or theirs. It's ours, the messy way we try to belong while outrunning our pain.

We're in a reckoning, whether we RSVP'd or not. Men are hurting. Women are hurting. Everyone's lugging programming and shame through the TSA of love, hoping we won't get flagged. We're trying to love each other without knowing how to love ourselves.

I didn't set out to become a Dick Fixer. A Wiener Whisperer. A Penis Peacemaker. A Shlong Shaman. But somehow, that's where I landed. And along the way I became something else: a witness to grief, to shame, to the quiet, terrifying, beautiful work of healing. One awkward conversation, one stubborn penis pump, one aging man with a hopeful heart at a time.

Somewhere in the middle of all that dick fixing... I found my own metaphorical dick. My agency. My core. My voice. Still a work in progress, sure, but mine, nonetheless.

Now that you do know a little more about dicks than you expected, I hope you'll join me in bridging the chasm between toxic masculinity and toxic femininity. We need curiosity, compassion, and better tools more than ever. I believe we can get there, one healed dick or dick lover at a time.

And lastly, maybe most importantly: if you have a dick, love a dick, or know someone who's got a dick... take care of it. Maybe that means buying a penis pump (you'll thank me later). Mostly it means tending the tender parts you'd rather hide, the ones you call weak, the ones that actually make you whole.

Because in the end, this story was never just about dicks. It was about the messy, terrifying, gorgeous work of mending what we were sure was unfixable. If a clinic full of broken dicks could teach me that, then I promise: you can find your way back to yourself, too.

Dicks, dicks, dicks! 362 dicks in this book, and still, I've held more in my hand. Can't wait to shake yours.

ACKNOWLEDGMENTS

Writing this book cracked me open in ways I never expected. It demanded truth over comfort, authenticity over performance, and the kind of courage I had to grow into one page at a time. I excavated and mined every corner of my heart, my history, and my psyche to tell this story honestly, to honor what was real, even when it was painful, complicated, or unflattering. Revisiting these parts of my life was not easy, but it mattered. And I didn't do it alone.

Dad - you are the complicated, infuriating, unforgettable heartbeat inside these pages. Loving you and losing you shaped everything I became. Thank you for my wit, my curiosity, and my fire. I hope somewhere you're smirking at the fact that your daughter wrote this book.

Mama - thank you for letting me process aloud with you every single day. For holding space for the messy parts, for the shared grief, for the rage, the softness, the stories, and the breakthroughs. I learned compassion, strength, and survival from you.

To my sisters - my first friends, my fiercest allies, and the reason I can find humor inside chaos. Thank you for being my lifelong witnesses. I love you.

To my husband, JoJo - thank you for standing with me in the shadows and the light. For loving me through the evolution, through the writing, through the unraveling, through the rebuilding and the lack of bathing to meet my deadlines. Your courage to face yourself inspires mine.

To my therapist, Jenn - thank you for letting me be an absolute mess with you. For honoring every part of me that needed to tell this story. For seeing me clearly at the exact moment I needed to be seen and being an endless resource of compassion. You walked into my life with divine timing.

To my cousin Hans, my artistic soulmate - your guidance, support, accountability, and emotional clarity were irreplaceable. Thank you for being a grounding force in the middle of creative chaos for this book and

so many other projects.

To Annie - my fierce mentor and friend. Thank you for believing in me long before I did. Your faith in me helped build the foundation this book stands on. Your incredible courage has fueled my career from day one. Thank you for being there through every career milestone.

To my Storyteller Media family - thank you for championing this book with conviction and heart.

To Charles Allen, my publisher - thank you for your consistent encouragement, your belief, and for taking a risk on this first-time author. You saw the potential in my vision before I could. You held it steady until I did. Thank you for being an incredible example of a fully embodied safe leader and man.

To Makena Metz, my brilliant editor - thank you for your insight, your humor, your precision, and every push that made this book sharper, deeper, and truer. I am a better writer because of you.

To the Macmillan sales and distribution team - thank you for carrying this book into the hands of readers with such care and enthusiasm.

To Ben Ceccarelli - my incredible friend and the genius behind my book cover. Your cheerleading, your creativity, and your perfectly timed dad jokes are one of the reasons I'm here. Thank you for pouring your heart into this with me.

To my early readers and champions, Traci, Tori, Karla, Beef, Gacky, Chase and Michaela. Thank you for holding these pages with tenderness, honesty, and enthusiasm. Your messages, voice notes, tears, laughter, and encouragement helped me trust this book in its most vulnerable form. You reminded me, over and over again, that this story mattered long before it ever reached the world.

To the men at The Clinic - thank you for trusting me with your stories, your fears, your hopes, your vulnerability... and, of course, your dicks. You taught me more about men, shame, intimacy, and healing than any class or therapist ever could. I carry each of you with me.

To my friends, my chosen family - thank you for feeding me, listening to me, loving me, laughing with me, and letting me collapse on your couches when the writing got too real. Your belief in me kept this book alive.

And finally, to the reader - thank you for picking up this book. Thank you for being brave enough to walk into this conversation. Thank you for holding space for the messy, complicated truth of being human. My deepest hope is that these pages made you feel seen, understood, and a little less alone.

This book is for all of us learning to heal the parts we were taught to hide.